ENDO

"Each devotional points to the Lord and invites the readers to seek Him more. While reading this devotional, it will stir your faith and encourage you daily. Let God speak to you through the words in *Powerful Whispers*!"

Rob Ketterling, Lead Pastor, River Valley Church

"*Powerful Whispers* is unlike any other devotional I have read. Not only does it give you practical and tangible steps each day to advance your heart towards God, it conveys a beautifully articulated picture of God's heart for you! It is virtually impossible for you not to be ushered into the presence of the Almighty God when you pick up this book! I most definitely plan to get this in the hands of all my loved ones and those who have yet to encounter the love of Jesus Christ!"

Tracy Smith, Licensed Minister of the Gospel

"This is such a great self-processing, devotional book. I can almost feel the heart of the writer day by day. Christa exemplifies humility, wisdom, integrity, and anointing within each day's devotion. Christa understands the heart of each woman, and she is able to see how God sees them. This book will impact many hearts that are diving deeper in their relationship with Christ."

Sarah Vanornum, Founder of All in Worship

Powerful Whispers

Christa Joy Spaeth

Cover Photo by Zac Gudakov on Unsplash

Cover and Interior Design by Dugan Design Group

Printed in the United States

ISBN 978-0-578-28801-7

Dedication

To my sons, Cody and Adam,
may the words written here be
a legacy you enjoy with
your families.
I pray you both continue to
be a light shining for Jesus.

I love you boys,

—Mom

Acknowledgments

First and foremost, I am thankful to the Lord for laying on my heart the desire and inspiration to write this book. A special thank you to my husband, Dave, for all your support and daily encouragement. Thank you for spending many hours reading and re-reading the contents and providing your insights. Thank you to my sons, Cody and Adam, for your excitement and encouragement to me, and willingness to be examples in the devotional. Thank you, Mom, for helping me craft the content into a great flow and for talking me through my last-minute questions. Thank you, Dad, for answering the last-minute texts I had! Thank you, Terry and Linda Dugan, for your kindness and insights to help prepare me for my first book launch.

A huge thank you to my GROW girlfriends, without you this book wouldn't be the same. What an amazing journey it has been since we met virtually in 2020. You have all become like family to me. We have laughed, cried, prayed, and shared life together. I am thankful for your deeply inspirational and heartfelt contributions to this book. The depth of your love for the Lord is inspiring. Your openness to share struggles and triumphs blessed me, and I know they will bless the readers.

Thank you to Roma Waterman for being my inspiration for writing. Your Heartsong Prophetic Alliance school was the pivotal linchpin that catapulted me into creating this book! A very sincere thank you to Nate and Christy Johnston for your faithfulness in launching the GROW group. Because of your guidance, I was able to grow in hearing from the Lord in a whole new way. Also, because of your group, I was able to meet my incredible GROW girlfriends.

Thank you to my dear friends and family who supported me financially and with prayers. Your sacrifice for this project is humbling and inspiring.

Contents

Week Six: God's Peace for You

Week Seven: The God Who Whispers

Introduction

Welcome! I am so glad you chose this book to be part of your journey. I have prayed for months this book will bless you and help you uncover God's heart for you. During the next seven weeks, may you grow closer to God and uncover His desire to know you more while you get to know Him more.

In 2020, when the world was in lockdown, as an introvert I found myself excited to spend more time at home. I was finally able to have extra time dedicated to morning devotions before starting my workday in my basement. My two-year journey has drawn me closer to God, and I want to share with you some of the beauty God has shown me. The Lord quickly started sharing His heart for His family and wanted me to share His words with you.

This devotional is different than most as it includes two important components. The first is special words from the heart of God for you. The second is suggested worship music to soak in God's love and greatness daily. I pray you can easily access a music streaming service to locate these songs as it is a key element. Music has meant so much to me, especially in the past two years, and I pray you find that music brings you closer to the heart of the Lord for you.

My inspirational verses for this devotional include:

- What I say to you in the dark, repeat in broad daylight, and what you hear in a whisper, announce it publicly *(Matthew 10:27 TPT)*.
- Trust in the Lord completely, and do not rely on your own opinions. With all your heart rely on him to guide you, and he will lead you in every decision you make. Become intimate with him in whatever you do, and he will lead you wherever you go *(Proverbs 3:5-6 TPT)*.

I pray your trust, love, and knowledge of the Lord's love for you grow during the upcoming seven weeks.

May God bless you greatly on this journey,

Christa Joy

Do You Know Jesus?

If you were to die today, do you know without a shadow of a doubt you would be going to heaven? If you are not sure, please continue reading and learn how to have secure knowledge you will be going to heaven.

To accept Jesus in your heart and make Him the Lord and Savior of your life, you first need to recognize there is no amount of religion, acts of kindness, or money that can get you into heaven. Jesus said, "I am the way, the truth, and the life. No one comes to the Father except through Me" *(John 14:6, NKJV)*.

God loved us so much that He sent His one and only son, Jesus, to die the death that we deserve and give us everything Jesus deserves, which is everlasting life. Jesus' sacrifice is more than enough for us: "For God so loved the world that he gave his one and only Son, that whoever believes in him shall not perish but have eternal life" *(John 3:16, NIV)*.

If you make this decision to accept Jesus as your Savior, your old life will pass away, and you will step victorious into a new life with Christ. *Romans 10:9-10* says, "If you declare with your mouth, 'Jesus is Lord,' and believe in your heart that God raised him from the dead, you will be saved. For it is with your heart that you believe and are justified, and it is with your mouth that you profess your faith and are saved" (NIV). Believe in your heart now and profess with your tongue the following:

> *Dear Jesus, I know that I have sinned. Please forgive me today. I receive the free gift of salvation. Today I choose to follow You for the rest of my life. Amen!*

If you said this prayer today, I want to say welcome to the family of Christ! You can rest assured that your prayer has been heard: "Everyone who calls on the name of the Lord will be saved" *(Acts 2:21, NIV)*. The simple next step I want to encourage you to do is tell someone of your life-changing decision. Connect with a Christian friend or family member, or call your local church and share the news. Also, I would be honored if you shared your decision with me. You can go to my website www.christajoyministries.com or send me an email at christajoyministries@gmail.com.

Outline of Each Devotional:

My desire with *Powerful Whispers* is to help you, dear reader, get a glimpse of how awe-inspiring God's whispers of His love are for you. He knows you, loves you, and fights for you daily. Each devotion shares God's heart for you.

The daily devotionals are comprised of the following sections:

Verses: The Scripture says to renew your minds (Romans 12:2), so we set each day firmly in the precious words written in the Bible. A variety of Bible versions are used throughout this book, each version is designated with appropriate abbreviations.

God's Whisper: The Lord is so kind and loving. He whispered these daily words to be written down, especially for you. Receive the encouraging words and know you are reading this book because the Lord wanted you to be blessed.

Personal: This section provides a variety of topics from each author, from personal and inspirational stories to digging into Bible stories related to each day's topic.

Suggested Worship: The term *praise* is mentioned 259 times in the Bible, and worship is mentioned 188 times.[1] This indicates how important worship is to God. God doesn't need our worship, but He wants us to worship and delights in our worship. For each daily devotion, I have provided at least one musical suggestion for worship. I strongly encourage you to seek these songs out on whatever platform you access music.

Activation: Each day's devotion provides a simple exercise to help engage your body and mind to cement the teaching in a new way.

Prayer: I encourage you to read each prayer as though you wrote it. Have an open heart to hear the Lord while you pray. I encourage the written prayer to be a starting point for you to expand on with your own words as you feel led.

My Reflection: Use this space to reflect on what spoke to your heart each day and what you heard God say to you. Finish each devotional with your personal prayer to the Lord.

---

[1] "Word Counts: How Many Times Does a Word Appear in the Bible." *Truth in Reality*, 8 Apr 2013, https://truthinreality.com/2013/04/08/word-counts-how-many-times-does-a-word-appear-in-the-bible/. Accessed 19 March, 2022.

WEEK ONE

God Knows You

I have never called you 'servants,' because a master doesn't confide in his servants, and servants don't always understand what the master is doing. But I call you my most intimate and cherished friends, for I reveal to you everything that I've heard from my Father.

John 15:15 (TPT)

1. You Are His Reflection

Verses:

- *Hebrews 1:3a (TPT):* "The Son is the dazzling radiance of God's splendor, the exact expression of God's true nature—his mirror image!"
- *2 Corinthians 3:18b (TPT):* "With no veil we all become like mirrors who brightly reflect the glory of the Lord Jesus. We are being transfigured into his very image as we move from one brighter level of glory to another. And this glorious transfiguration comes from the Lord, who is the Spirit."

God's Whisper:

I will fill you up with favor for I have called you. I have formed you in your mother's womb. Be patient I have great things in store for you. Let wonder fill your eyes, My child. I am setting in place angels to surround and protect you. You have a great purpose ahead filled with joy. Smile My child, smile for I am with you always. I will comfort you.

Personal:

I am humbled that we are being transfigured into Jesus' image, who is Himself the mirror image of God—wow! I was born with a cleft lip and had two surgeries to fix the defect. While the doctors had amazing skill and patched me up quite well, I still have a scar on my lip and a little bit of a crooked nose. I was sure my nose was all anyone saw when they met me. When I was younger, I even asked for God to heal me so I could be "normal."

Being healed was not the path the Lord had for me, but through my uniqueness, I found how others with similar life experiences had been drawn to me. I didn't appreciate this connection early on, but I now realize that what I thought were my imperfections was a chance to connect with and minister to others. Today I can say, thank You God for making me how You have made me, for Your ways are higher than my ways, and Your plans for me are perfect. I can echo the psalmist and sing, "I praise you because I am fearfully and wonderfully made; your works are wonderful; I know that full well" *(Psalm 139:14, NIV)*.

Suggested Worship:

"Psalm 139 (Far Too Wonderful)" by Shane & Shane

Activation:

Take a look at your face in the mirror and smile! Recognize that God created you, and every wrinkle you have and every imperfection you may think you see is truly beautiful to God. Thank Him for creating you and molding you in His image. Ask God to help you love any "imperfection" you see. He will help you because He loves you, every bit of you.

Prayer: Dear Lord, I'm sorry I am critical of how I look sometimes. Forgive me, Father, and cleanse me of my negative thoughts about myself. Help me to be thankful for how You created me. Help me to fall in love with every little bit of me that You created. Thank You, Father, that You created me and that I am fearfully and wonderfully made. Amen.

My Reflection:

2. God Is Your Friend

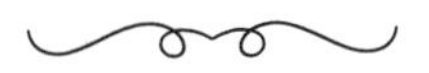

Verse:

- *John 15:15 (TPT)* "I have never called you 'servants,' because a master doesn't confide in his servants, and servants don't always understand what the master is doing. But I call you my most intimate and cherished friends, for I reveal to you everything that I've heard from my Father."

God's Whisper:

I am your friend, and I want to show you great wonders I have hidden in your heart. When you spend time with Me, I will work to unravel the secrets I have hidden just for you. Remember, My child, to knock and the door will be opened, ask and it will be given unto you, seek and you will find, with Me as your guide. Let Me work in and through you. My arms are open wide to hug you and give you rest and comfort, so run to Me now. I love you and call you My friend.

Personal:

When I think of a friend, I think of long coffee chats or extended evenings laughing in front of a fireplace. Did you know that is what Jesus loves to do with you too? He loves to sit and chat and hear about your day. The Lord loves to laugh! God's people are meant to laugh; we aren't supposed to be solemn. We are to be joyous as He is joyous!

An amazing miracle happened in the Bible when a very elderly couple, Sarah and Abraham, were blessed with the birth of their son Isaac. About this, Sarah said, "God has brought me laughter, and everyone who hears about this will laugh with me" *(Genesis 21:6, NIV)*. Laugh today, for the Lord is your friend, and He is doing great and mighty things in your life.

Suggested Worship:

"Joy of the Lord" by Micah Dillon

Activation:

Spend time alone with God now. Set a timer for three minutes and ask God what secrets He has hidden for you. Write out what you hear or draw a picture in this space of what He shows you. For me, God often shows me flowers. I take note of the type of flower and the color, and then later I love to go deeper and find out the meaning of what He shows me, I use various Christian resource books to help me understand meanings of items the Lord shares with me. Ask Him and listen.

Prayer: Lord, I am so thankful You are my friend. Let me be reminded of Your friendship daily and come to You with the same things I do and say with my earthly friends, and even more. Help me to come to You and share all my joy and silly stories, not just my sorrows. Let my heart be open to all You are and relish in Your love and kindness. Amen.

My Reflection:

3. God Oversees Your Soul

Verses:

- *Psalm 121:1-2 (TPT)* "I look up to the mountains and hills, longing for God's help. But then I realize that our true help and protection is only from the Lord, our Creator who made the heavens and the earth."

God's Whisper:

Hear me, O child, for I have come to save you. Hear My heartbeat for you. I long to hold you close. Come to Me, My child, I have the key to unlock the mysteries of your heart. I cherish you and watch over your precious soul with tender and loving care.

Personal:

I recently had a vision of a boy, barefoot and standing in the sand on a calm beach, looking up into the clouds at the setting sun. The boy suddenly saw the Lord's hands reaching down. The Lord was holding a beautiful heart, the boy's heart. The heart had a lock on it. The Lord was saying, "Come to Me child, I have the key to unlock the mysteries of your heart."

Reflecting on this vision, I am reminded of the verse, "It is the glory of God to conceal a matter; to search out a matter is the glory of kings" *(Proverbs 25:2, NIV)*. God loves you so much that He wants you to spend time with Him searching out the great treasures He has hidden just for you. Put aside extra time for Him and rest in Him and Him alone. Come to the Lord as a child as it says in Matthew 18:3. Come to Him innocent, full of wonder and excitement to be with Him. Be like a child on Christmas morning, eager to open good presents from your parents. Imagine that the Lord has even better gifts in store for you. Not only does the Lord oversee your soul, He knows you so intimately that He wants to share and unlock mysteries He has planted in your heart. Trust in the Lord with all your heart, soul, mind, and strength, and He will share the mysteries with you.

Suggested Worship:

"You Know Me" by Steffany Gretzinger, Bethel Music Worship

Activation:

Ask the Lord what mysteries He wants to uncover in you. Spend two minutes writing down these mysteries. If you don't hear or have a sense of any mysteries today, write down your secret desires and ask the Lord to reveal if these are His heart's desires for you.

Prayer: I am so in awe of You, Lord. I am asking You today to unlock the mysteries of Your heart for me so I can explore them. I know the mysteries will be perfect because You know every part of my being, for You created me. Amen.

My Reflection:

4. God Sets You Apart

KRISTIN KURTZ

Verse:

- *Leviticus 20:26 (NLT)* "You must be holy because I, the Lord, am holy. I have set you apart from all other people to be my very own."

God's Whisper:

I see your face, My child. I see Me reflected in your eyes. Thank You for seeking Me and putting aside the noise of the world. Stay focused on Me now for I have set you apart to live in My glory. Stay near Me, precious one, for the road may be bumpy at times but I am here to carry you on the path I have called you to be on.

Personal:

The world will attempt to pull you off the path God has for you. Stay on that narrow path. God has designed a blueprint and map perfect for you. Stay focused on Jesus— keeping your eyes up. Keep from looking side to side. Distraction lurks all around you where you will get lost and comparison will set in. Do a chin check and look up to God, child.

Suggested Worship:

"Set Apart" featuring Citylight Worship by Harvester Worship

Activation:

Fully embrace who He has called you to be, a set-apart child of the Most High. Speak out loud three times, "I AM a masterpiece, chosen, and I will BOLDLY go where He leads me.

Prayer: Father, remind me who I am through Your redeeming power working in me. Show me the unique ways You have created me to do mighty works for Your GLORY! Amen!

My Reflection:

5. The Good Shepherd Who Knows You

Verses:

- *Psalm 23:2-3 (TPT):* "He offers a resting place for me in his luxurious love. His tracks take me to an oasis of peace near the quiet brook of bliss. That's where he restores and revives my life. He opens before me the right path and leads me along in his footsteps of righteousness so that I can bring honor to his name."
- *John 10:27 (NIV):* "My sheep listen to my voice; I know them, and they follow me."

God's Whisper:

I am the Good Shepherd, let Me lead you. I have only good plans for you. I love you, My child. I will open pathways for you. I will make your ways easy. Lean on Me today. Listen to Me, and I will guide you and carry you through all the tough times. I will never leave you. I will give you rest.

Personal:

The Lord is watching over you, protecting you. He will always search you out if you are lost. The staff in the Good Shepherd's hand is used to protect the sheep from anything that would hurt them. So be comforted in His protection. The Lord is near to heal you, nurture you, and show you how a true Shepherd treats His sheep. As it says in Psalms 28:9b (TPT), "Be our shepherd leading us forward, forever carrying us in your arms!"

Listen to the Lord, it may be hard in this noisy world but quiet yourself and get to know His voice. To help quiet your mind, think about the "oasis of peace" He leads you to, the "quiet brook of bliss." Close your eyes and imagine this place of refuge. Ask the Lord to speak to you in the quietness. The Lord speaks truth and love, not condemnation or fear. The Lord loves you. He is the Good Shepherd.

Suggested Worship:

"Shepherd" by Amanda Cook, Bethel Music

Activation:

Read Psalm 23 in two translations to obtain a fresh perspective on this encouraging psalm. Pick a verse that speaks the most to you, write it down, and refer to the verse throughout the day. Thank God for His goodness of being your Good Shepherd.

Prayer: Lord, thank You for being my Good Shepherd. I rest in knowing You have only good plans for me. Take my hand and help me learn what those plans are. Help me walk on the path you have set before me. For as it states in Psalm 23, why would I fear the future if only goodness and tender love pursue me? Thank You, Jesus. Amen.

My Reflection:

6. God Is Working in You

Verse:

- *Philippians 2:13 (TPT):* "God will continually revitalize you, implanting within you the passion to do what pleases him."

God's Whisper:

I am always working in you, My child. Give Me your heart today. Focus on My voice, and I will kindle in you great passion for things of value in this world. The passion may be for things that you put aside years ago, or things new to you. I will ignite a passion for things that please Me while using your talents. I will bless you greatly to use these skills I created in you, and these skills will give Me glory and honor while invigorating you.

Personal:

My son, Cody, had a dream from the Lord when he was 13 to be a rescue diver for the Coast Guard. He worked hard towards that goal by swimming hundreds of hours every year. In addition, he became a swim instructor, a first aid responder, and worked at a marina. He enlisted in the Coast Guard shortly after high school where he continued to work towards qualifying for his dream. When he went to his final physical for the rescue diving program, he was declined due to an unknown color blindness. Cody was devastated that his dream didn't come true.

He took one weekend to be sad, and then come Monday, he turned toward his next passion of being a U.S. Coast Guard Damage

Controlman. He easily got into that program and graduated. At graduation, a fellow shipmate came up to me and said, "Cody has such love for Jesus!" I discovered Cody had spent many nights praying and talking with this young man and others. As a mom, I was so proud, but more importantly, I could see right away that Cody was in the right place for his light to shine for Jesus for those around him.

Dreams may not always come true how you would desire or expect them to, but rest assured that when you give God your plans, He will refresh you and share His plans for you. God may not share more than one small next step, but have faith He is working in you. As Paul wrote in Romans, "we know that all things work together for good to those who love God, to those who are called according to His purpose" (Romans 8:28, NKJV).

Suggested Worship:

"God's Not Done with You" by Tauren Wells

Activation:

Set a timer and spend two minutes writing down your talents, passions, and desires. Ask the Lord how He wants to use these gifts and write down your sense of His response.

Prayer: Dear Lord, I pray Philippians 2:13 over me today. I am so thankful You want to continually refresh me. Lord, some days it's hard to feel that I am restored. I wake up groggy, worried I have missed Your desire for my life, and sometimes discouraged I will never accomplish my dream. Please show me what You want for me to do today, this week, and this month using my passions to bring You glory. Amen.

My Reflection:

7. God Sees You

TERESA KRAFFT

Verse:

- *Genesis 16:13 (NKJV):* "Then she called the name of the Lord who spoke to her, You-Are-the-God-Who-Sees; for she said, 'Have I also here seen Him who sees me?'"

God's Whisper:

Child, I live inside of you and am with you always. I see you when you are staring in the mirror and struggling to find a glimpse of Me within yourself. Call on My name. Look into My eyes and see Me. Remember that I am your God, and I SEE and HEAR and RESCUE you from every prison, from the wilderness. Always remember I love you, dear child.

Personal:

For most of my childhood, the enemy would attack in hidden places, making me feel invisible, unseen, and my pain was deeply embedded. My voice muted several times, I had even wished the pain would be more visible, but somehow, it always disappeared deep inside. I didn't know then that the Lord sees my pain.

The Lord gave me, through the passing of my mother-in-law, a precious ruby ring that I wear every day because it reminds me of being His Bride. I love that it's more "fancy" than I would have picked for myself. It's a visible reminder of the gold He calls out of me. It's also a reminder of a dream I had several years ago where He called out the invisible me and had me use my voice. In the dream, I had been bloodied and was being brought into prison. As a group was about to do more harm to me, I lifted my right arm and hand to the sky, and noticing that

I was wearing a signet ring, cried out, "I am royalty, and I have summoned my King and He is coming to rescue me!" The right hand[2] and signet ring[3] both symbolize authority.

In a moment of deep pain, when I had lost hope, I recall standing in front of the mirror. Looking deep into my eyes with tears streaming down my face, I searched for the Lord. I knew He was inside of me, and I clung to that remaining hope. I remember saying out loud, "I KNOW YOU SEE ME!!" I would not let go of that. In our most difficult seasons, where the enemy of our soul wants to imprison us again, we can take authority and lift our voice to HIM.

Suggested Worship:

"The God Who Sees" by The Rock, The Road, and The Rabbi Foundation

Activation:

Step out of the worry, the time crunch, and pause to reflect on the fact that God sees you. In the sweetness of this quiet moment, it's no longer about what you do or what you need to do. Take a look in the mirror and imagine the beauty that God sees in you. Pause and ask God to show you what He sees. He will restore your peace. He will bring rest to your soul. HE SEES YOU.

Prayer: Lord, I ask that You call me to the stillness of Your presence today, to KNOW that YOU ARE GOD and all that comes with that. May I receive YOUR REST in knowing all will be well. In Jesus' name. Amen.

---

[2] Exodus 15:6 (ESV): "Your right hand, O LORD, glorious in power, your right hand, O LORD, shatters the enemy."

[3] Esther 8:8 (ESV): "But you may write as you please with regard to the Jews, in the name of the king, and seal it with the king's ring, for an edict written in the name of the king and sealed with the king's ring cannot be revoked."

My Reflection:

WEEK TWO

God Loves You

The Lord appeared to us in the past, saying: "I have loved you with an everlasting love; I have drawn you with unfailing kindness."

Jeremiah 31:3 (NIV)

1. God Forgives

Verses:

- *Psalm 32:2-3 & 5 (TPT):* "What bliss belongs to those who have confessed their corruption to God! For he wipes their slates clean and removes hypocrisy from their hearts. Before I confessed my sins, I kept it all inside; my dishonesty devastated my inner life, causing my life to be filled with frustration, irrepressible anguish, and misery. . . . Then I finally admitted to you all my sins, refusing to hide them any longer. I said, 'My life-giving God, I will openly acknowledge my evil actions.' And you forgave me! All at once, the guilt of my sin washed away and all my pain disappeared!"

- *1 John 1:9 (NIV):* "If we confess our sins, he is faithful and just and will forgive us our sins and purify us from all unrighteousness."

God's Whisper:

Listen to Me, My child, let Me tell you a story. Once upon a time, there was a man, a sinful man who came before Me. He knew of Me but didn't worship Me. I asked him to have a picnic with Me so I could share My heart for him. The man wept once he knew how much I loved him. After that moment, he asked for forgiveness and I washed him with My great love, forgiving him of everything. He had new freedom he never had before. He was happy! He grew to know Me more deeply as we walked and talked together daily. My child, I ask you today, spend time with Me and only Me like the man in this story. I will show you wonders, great wonders about how I love you.

Personal:

A few years ago, after I reinstated regular daily devotions and was closer to the Lord, the devil tried to remind me of my sins that occurred over 30 years before and tell me I was not worthy. I found myself thinking constantly about the cheating in school I did so many years ago even though I had totally forgotten about it for decades. I felt sick to my stomach that I had actually done something so incredibly irresponsible and stupid. The enemy continued to tell me God hadn't forgiven me of those sins. I was tormented thinking about my mistakes for several weeks, during which I was continually asking God for forgiveness but not feeling or believing I had received it. When the torment continued, I asked my husband and others to pray with me. Still, the guilt was heavy and weighing me down; it was hard to think of anything else.

One day, I finally allowed the scriptures above to sink in and be real to my life. God said if we confess our sins, then He forgives! I finally realized the devil's claims were false, and I started to claim Jesus' victory over all sin and believe that I had been forgiven. The burden was lifted off of me. I felt Jesus wipe the slate clean! Hallelujah!

God doesn't think about my sin anymore nor does He think of any of your sins ever again. Believe you can live free in the Lord, for He has forgiven you!

Suggested Worship:

"East to West" by River Valley Worship

Activation:

Write down on a small piece of paper any sins you need forgiveness for. Ask God to forgive you of your sins and thank Him for forgiving you. Tear up your paper and toss it in a garbage can. Proclaim, "God has forgiven me, and I don't need to think of those sins anymore."

Prayer: Dear Jesus, thank You for forgiving me of all my sins. I thank You for washing me clean so I can start fresh today in Your great love. Help me to remember this always and know Your forgiveness to be true deep in my heart. I look forward to being closer to You each day and having greater freedom in Your love for me. Amen.

My Reflection:

2. God's Perspective of You

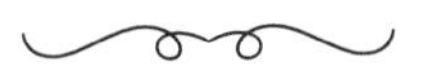

Verses:

- *Ephesians 3:18-19 (TPT):* "Then you will be empowered to discover what every holy one experiences—the great magnitude of the astonishing love of Christ in all its dimensions. How deeply intimate and far-reaching is his love! How enduring and inclusive it is! Endless love beyond measurement that transcends our understanding—this extravagant love pours into you until you are filled to overflowing with the fullness of God!"

God's Whisper:

I have called you by name, My child. I created you and know every fiber of your being. I loved you before you were born, and My heart thrills when you spend time with Me. I love to hear your thoughts; you are so creative! I love to hear the desires of your heart; share them with Me more often. Please sit with Me today. I miss you some days. I am always here waiting for you to come talk to Me and just be quiet in My presence. I don't ask you for anything, but I do desire your willingness to spend time with Me. Let Me show you My perspective of you. I have a wonderful story I am creating in heaven of your journey on earth. I will show you how I was there by your side always. I love you so.

Personal:

Last fall, while on a walk on a beautiful sunny day, I decided to wear my polarized, prescription sunglasses. The Lord gave me a revelation that my view of the world while wearing sunglasses—as opposed to squinting, half-blinded by the sun—was like looking at the world from God's perspective. I noticed when I looked up in the trees that the leaves were more colorful, brighter. I noticed a depth of beauty in the wooded forest, with more definition in the trees than I could see with my naked eye. This, I thought, is how God sees me. The verse above from Ephesians that says "the great magnitude of the astonishing love of Christ in all its dimensions" came to light in a new way. The Lord loves us more and deeper than I can even imagine. The Lord wants you to look at yourself from His perspective. He sees so much beauty in you, more than you can see when you look at yourself.

Suggested Worship:

"Jesus Lover of My Soul" by Awakening Music, featuring Daniel Hagen

Activation:

Ask God to show you how He sees you from His perspective—seeing you as more beautiful than you can imagine. Write it down and place it in your Bible to remind yourself how God sees and loves you. Ask Him to help change your perspective of yourself and make it more like God's view of you. Remember, you are loved by the Creator of the universe!

Prayer: God, thank You for being the lover of my soul. Change my perspective. Give me Your vision of how You see me and how You love me. I want to know You more today. I want to give You my all, for You loved me before I was born and created me for Your glory. Thank You for being my best friend. No one can love me like You do. Amen.

My Reflection:

3. God Designed You

with LESLIE SCHEWE

Verse:

- *Isaiah 64:8 (NKJV):* "But now, O Lord, You are our Father; We are the clay, and You our potter; and all we are the work of Your hand."

God's Whisper:

I am the Lord your God. I have molded you so carefully from before your conception. You are My treasure. Let me continue to mold you. I can soften your heart in areas you thought were long ago hardened. My purpose for you here on earth is extraordinary. All I ask is for you to rest in Me, believe in Me, and I will continue to craft a beautiful story in you.

Personal:

Design; Designer. Created; Creator. Clay; Potter. Child; Father.

Friend, meditate today on the fact that you are someone who was created intentionally. You were carefully designed for a divine purpose. You are unique, a one-of-a-kind creation. The Great Potter skillfully, deliberately, and lovingly molds you. Give way to His gentle hands, knowing you are secure in Him. He may do some reshaping or fine-tuning of the beautiful details, but He always and only makes masterpieces.

Suggested Worship:

"Canvas and Clay" by Bryan and Katie Torwalt

Activation:

God uniquely made each of us. Today choose at least one of the activations that best speaks to you.

- Think about something you used to love doing when you were a child or something you used to do and have stopped. Pick it up again.
- Think about something that makes you unique and allow it to make you SMILE!
- What colors are you drawn to? Use those colors to paint, draw, or color a picture that represents YOU!

Prayer: Lord, thank You for creating me. I am humbled that You created me to be a masterpiece. May I live today walking out the path You have for me, delighting in my unique design. I ask that You show me the details of the day You want me to live out. Amen.

My Reflection:

4. God Works All Things for Good

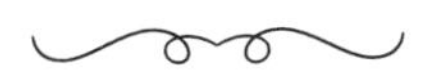

Verses:

- *Romans 8:28 (NKJV):* "And we know that all things work together for good to those who love God, to those who are the called according to His purpose."
- *Psalm 8:1 (TPT):* "Yahweh, our Sovereign God, your glory streams from the heavens above, filling the earth with the majesty of your name! *People everywhere see your splendor.*"

God's Whisper:

My dear child, give Me your heart, and I will open up the heavens to you. I want only what is good for you. Trust Me, worship Me, for I am a good God. I love you and want what's best for you. Remember, love is from Me, for I am love. Hear My words today and be blessed.

Personal:

I have a type A personality, at work and at home. I am a list maker, a task master (just ask my husband), always aiming to get a large number of tasks done in as short a time as possible. Also, if projects do not get done in the timely manner I decided on, I get a little flustered. I want things done according to my timelines. Over the years, I've found that this controlling personality type doesn't lend to a good relationship with the Lord. In my imperfectness, I must consciously give control to God. When I started to let go of my timelines and trust in Him, I found peace. It was a dramatic shift when I finally trusted God,

I've had great peace knowing that He works all things in His timing! I wish it wouldn't have taken me so long to realize this!

Each morning, I try to pray and tell the Lord that I lay down my plans and my burdens at His feet because He knows what is best for me. I have found journaling, which is new to me, has been a simple way to record how I see Him moving daily. On days I don't feel or hear anything from God, I still believe the scriptures above are true, and I stand on the knowledge that God is loving. I am humbled to know God is ALWAYS working good for me. Simply put, God controls all things with His mighty love, and thus I know the best is yet to come when walking daily with Him, even if things aren't going according to my plan.

Suggested Worship:

"Psalm 8 (How Majestic Is Your Name)" by Shane & Shane

Activation:

In an act of submission to lay down your burdens to God, write down areas of your life where you find yourself grasping for control, areas in which you want to trust God more. Maybe it's your health, your finances, your marriage. Grab a backpack and put the papers in the backpack and lay it down at your feet. If you use a planner, add it to the backpack. Let God know that you give Him all your worries, your plans, your day's schedule. Give it all to Him. Give Him the control of your life. He will bless you.

Prayer: Today, sovereign Lord, I lay all my plans at Your feet. I worship You now. I give You praise, honor, and glory. I entrust to You my heart and my desires, for I know You will work it all for good. Thank You, Lord, for loving me. Amen.

My Reflection:

5. *Your Protector*

Verses:

- *Psalm 91:14-15 (TPT):* "For here is what the Lord has spoken to me: 'Because you loved me, delighted in me, and have been loyal to my name, I will greatly protect you. I will answer your cry for help every time you pray, and you will feel my presence in your time of trouble. I will deliver you and bring you honor.'"

- *Deuteronomy 31:6 (NIV):* "Be strong and courageous. Do not be afraid or terrified because of them, for the Lord your God goes with you; he will never leave you nor forsake you."

God's Whisper:

I am here to protect you from all harm in the physical and spiritual realm. You don't know how many times I have guarded you against evil, but rest assured I am always with you. I am your safe harbor; the protector of your mind, heart, and spirit. I love you, My child.

Personal:

When I heard God's whisper today, I asked Him to remind me of a few times that He has protected me. I was reminded of a time in high school when I was crossing the street while talking to a friend and not paying attention to where I was going. All of a sudden, I was pulled backward by a different friend to escape being hit by a passing car that didn't see me. I believe we will be amazed in heaven to find out how many times the Lord was watching over us in similar situations, protecting us from physical harm when we didn't even realize He was there.

I was also reminded of times in high school and college where I was protected. People would tell me months later that they never invited me to drinking parties because I was "too innocent" and they didn't want to taint me. Honestly, at the time I was hurt not being invited to parties. I felt like an outsider, not fitting in. However, looking back, I can clearly see the Lord was protecting me from being exposed to things that may have led me down a path further from Him.

Dear friends, remember today's verse from Deuteronomy: God is always with you. When you're depressed, feel like an outsider, or are in trouble, He is there by your side. He hears you and sends His strength to encourage you. I have faith that you will look back years from now and see how the Lord has provided His protection. But even now, you can cry out to God to protect you. One powerful way to cry out is to pray scriptures out loud. Many theologians say speaking scripture out loud breaks spiritual bonds and forces the enemy to flee. I like to read scriptures of protection over my family. The chapters I most often choose are found in Psalm 91 and Psalm 23.

Suggested Worship:

"Protector" by Kim Walker-Smith

Activation:

Ask the Lord when He has protected you physically, mentally, or spiritually that you didn't even realize. Thank the Lord for all His protection. Consider reading Psalm 91 out loud as a blessing of protection over you and your family.

Prayer: Lord, I love you. Thank you for being my Protector, may You open my eyes to the times I didn't see You or feel Your presence. I am running to Your open arms today. May I always remember to honor You by reading from Your Word, the Bible, and to cry out to You, trusting in Your love and protection. Amen.

My Reflection:

6. The Lord, Your Healer

Verses:

- *Isaiah 53:4-5 (NIV):* "Surely he took up our pain and bore our suffering, yet we considered him punished by God, stricken by him, and afflicted. But he was pierced for our transgressions, he was crushed for our iniquities; the punishment that brought us peace was on him, and by his wounds, we are healed."
- *Ephesians 1:3 (NIV):* "Praise be to the God and Father of our Lord Jesus Christ, who has blessed us in the heavenly realms with every spiritual blessing in Christ."

God's Whisper:

I am here to heal you, My child. I don't want to heal only your body but also your soul. Get to know Me, the Great Physician. My son died for you and rose again to make you whole on earth. I proclaim mighty works will be done in you by simply accepting My gift of wholeness. Reach out to Me today, and I will lead you on the path to finding complete healing.

Personal:

When my youngest son, Adam, was born, I knew almost immediately he wasn't completely healthy. I remember at just three weeks old he would stare out the window. He never connected or bonded with my husband or me, never gazing into our eyes. At just four months of age, the doctors diagnosed him with autism. I wasn't surprised, yet I was devastated to hear this diagnosis on top of a few other physical ailments. We received the diagnosis on a Friday. My husband and I reached out to many friends and family members to pray that weekend. On Sunday night my husband prayed over our son to be healed, and as he prayed, our son let out a huge breath, and my husband knew that our son was healed at that moment. The next day we went back to the same doctor, and she was amazed at his change. She said she must have made a mistake in her diagnosis. We knew she didn't make a mistake; God performed a supernatural miracle that weekend! Praise the Lord!

I know God doesn't choose to heal everyone on this earth, but He does long for us to ask Him and rely on Him for all our hurts, whether we need physical, spiritual, or emotional healing. Reach out to Him. He is waiting to hear from you. I take comfort and joy knowing that our great Healer "Jesus Christ is the same yesterday, today, and forever" *(Hebrews 13:8, NKJV)*.

Suggested Worship:

Search the following compilation on YouTube: "20 minute deep prayer music / Prophetic Worship/Spontaneous Song / 'Rivers of Healing'" by Roma Waterman

Activation:

Spend time making a list of the healings you are trusting God to do for you and your family. Take time to pray for each prayer request. Proclaim in His mighty name you are healed and whole by the power of Jesus' name.

Prayer: Lord, thank You for being the Ultimate Healer. You said in Ephesians 1:3 that You have blessed us with every spiritual blessing in Christ. One of those blessings is being a healer. I pray You impart this healing on me and my family by the power of the precious blood of Jesus. I long to be touched by Your hand. Thank You that You are more than enough for me. Amen.

My Reflection:

7. God Is the Promise Keeper

TERESA KRAFFT

Verse:

- *1 Kings 8:24 (NKJV):* "You have kept what You promised Your servant David my father; You have both spoken with Your mouth and fulfilled it with Your hand, as it is this day."

God's Whisper:

I AM the promise keeper. I AM the author and finisher. You have created Ishmaels, places where you have been striving to birth promises on your own without Me. But these Ishmaels will now turn into Isaacs, My promises to you to be fulfilled in My perfect and set time. I SPOKE a WORD and you have walked with that promise through the wilderness. I knew the years and roads you would walk to arrive at this day. The journey itself is such a joy for Me, no matter the circumstances, and I now take you into the promise that awaits you. Even the promises you laid down—you can pick them up again. I'm a good, good Father who not only begins a thing but also completes it in you. What I have said to you, I WILL FULFILL—through you, with you, and in you.

Personal:

When I surrendered my heart to the Lord, He took me in a dream to a view He had in mind for me—the view was a promise. It was a Godly promise because I couldn't get there without Him. Little did I know as a new believer, there would be a journey with many trials. It was like seeing the end at the beginning of my road. In the years following, through every trial,

He picked me back up. If I tried to go home too soon, He sent me back, with some extra help to boot. He never left me. He never pressured or rushed me. Nearing the end of each "race," He told me, "There is NO rushing." There was a "wait" and a "rest" time too. He has calmed the panic with His "BE STILL AND KNOW!" I learned to trust. Rest. He is the finisher of every promise He births in you. You can count on it.

Suggested Worship:

"Way Maker" by Darlene Zschech & William McDowell

Activation:

Journal about the things He wants to do with you and things He has already started in and through you. What are the dreams He gave you—even as a child? Are there some you want to rekindle? Be still and know: He can do it. As you think about the dreams and promises, write them down, meditate on them and declare them to come to completion in His timing. There will be a launch, count on that too. Seek, praise, and worship Him. He is trustworthy—THE GREAT I AM—the promise keeper.

Prayer: Lord, I ask that You speak a word of encouragement to me today. Open my eyes and ears to hear You. Speak to me. Remind me of promises forgotten. Restore to me what the locusts have eaten. Help me to take simple steps towards completion and know that YOU ARE THE FINISHER, LORD. May it be according to Your will and Your timing, and Lord, cause me to be restful as I wait. In Jesus' name. Amen.

My Reflection:

WEEK THREE

God Fights for You

The Lord is my rock, my fortress and my deliverer; my God is my rock in whom I take refuge, my shield and the horn of my salvation, my stronghold.

Psalm 18:2 (NIV)

1. The Lord Our Rock

AMY HIRSH

Verses:

- *Psalm 18:2 (NIV):* "The Lord is my rock, my fortress and my deliverer; my God is my rock, in whom I take refuge, my shield and the horn of my salvation, my stronghold."
- *Deuteronomy 32:4 (NIV):* "He is the Rock, his works are perfect, and all his ways are just. A faithful God who does no wrong, upright and just is he."

God's Whisper:

When the troubles of this world drag you down, simply call out to Me, and I, the Lord your Rock, will lift you up to a high place, safe and secure before My face. I want you to know that, as the Lord your Rock, I am a mountain castle, a place of defense, a mighty citadel so strengthened the enemy cannot approach you here. It is the peak place of safety where you can find rest for your battle-weary soul. Instead of wearing yourself out trying to defend and protect yourself, trust I can and will defend you! Let go of everything weighing you down, and instead fly to the fortress available to you. I am waiting. In Me, the Lord your Rock, you will find ultimate escape.

Personal:

As a child growing up in a home with a lot of fighting, I often felt defenseless and without security. I felt like I was constantly exposed to the harshest elements of a storm and there was nowhere I could run for shelter. As I grew, that feeling of insecurity followed me for more years than I would care to admit. I found myself trying to control my circumstances to mitigate any possibility of dark clouds on the horizon. I thought if I tried harder, worked harder, gave more, stressed more, and performed more I could eliminate any turbulence and there would be peace. I'm sure you can imagine what came next. I found myself in a counselor's chair battling depression. I came to the end of myself and knew I had to change. As I learned to let go of my mountain of worry, I discovered God as my mountain of safety. Whenever worries would rise, or I was tempted to fight back against the opposition, my defense was to call on Him to hide me in His High Tower. As I did that, I came to know Him not only as my Rock but my Defender. As Exodus 14:14 (NIV) so beautifully says, "The Lord will fight for you; you need only be still." So beloved, if you're feeling exposed during the storms of life, you can ALWAYS find shelter in the Lord your Rock. Call to Him, and He will usher you right into His enduring strength.

Suggested Worship:

"Defender" by Jesus Culture

Activation:

Today, as you encounter any problems, big or small, instead of trying to "fix" them yourself, ask the Lord to help you solve them while you spend time in His shelter of safety.

Prayer: Lord, I declare You are my Rock, my Strong Shelter, where I can find refuge from anything life throws at me today. Thank You, God. You promise to lift me out of the enemy's sight. I release my cares to You today and trust You will defend me as I remain still and safe in Your mountain castle. I love You, Lord. Please give me a fresh, personal revelation of how You are the Lord, my Rock. Amen.

My Reflection:

2. Armed for Battle

Verses:

- *Psalms 24:7-9 (TPT):* "So wake up, you living gateways! Lift up your heads, you doorways of eternity! Welcome the King of Glory, for he is about to come through you. You ask, 'Who is this King of Glory?' Yahweh, armed and ready for battle, Yahweh, invincible in every way! So wake up, you living gateways, and rejoice! Fling wide, you eternal doors! Here he comes; the King of Glory is ready to come in."

God's Whisper:

I am ready to battle for you. Hear Me in the beat of My music. Know I am God and I conquer all. All will fall when I advance; know I advance for you. I am mighty and powerful, and I won't back down when I fight for you. Prepare yourself now and put on your full armor of God. Know I go before you always, wherever and whenever you go. Just call on Me. I will be there for you.

Personal:

God will fight for you, but He also wants you to be armed and ready also for the spiritual battles of this world. In Ephesians 6:12, we find the "struggle is not against flesh and blood, but against the rulers, against the authorities, against the powers of this dark world and against the spiritual forces of evil in the heavenly realms" (NIV). We need to be prepared to wage war against spiritual principalities. These battles can range from depression, condemnation, and guilt to desires of the flesh and so many others things.

Did you know that we are supposed to put on the full armor of God daily? In Ephesians 6:14-18 (TPT) we see the description of this armor:

> "Put on truth as a belt to strengthen you to stand in triumph. Put on holiness as the protective armor that covers your heart. Stand on your feet alert, then you'll always be ready to share the blessings of peace. In every battle, take faith as your wrap-around shield, for it is able to extinguish the blazing arrows coming at you from the evil one! Embrace the power of salvation's full deliverance, like a helmet to protect your thoughts from lies. And take the mighty razor-sharp Spirit-sword of the spoken word of God. Pray passionately in the Spirit, as you constantly intercede with every form of prayer at all times. Pray the blessings of God upon all his believers."

The Lord needs us to be engaged and active by putting on the full armor of God daily, so get up and make yourself battle-ready. As The Message translation of Psalm 24:7b says, "Wake up, you sleepyhead people. King-Glory is ready to enter." I start my day in prayer asking God to go before me and beside me and help me face another day as His warrior and vessel. In addition, I often get battle-ready before I go to sleep as I find that the enemy attacks me at night with thoughts of all I have done wrong that day and feelings of unworthiness. I find my best night's sleep is when I pray strong warrior-type prayers of protection and ask God to fight any spiritual warfare battles for me.

Suggested Worship:

"The God of Angel Armies" by Kelly Outzen

Activation:

Visualize putting on the full armor of God. I suggest writing out the above verses from Ephesians and putting them on a notecard in a room you commonly use as you start your day. It is so important to be suited up in God's armor each day. Practice this twice, in the morning and at night.

Prayer: Lord, use me like a mighty warrior in Your army fighting against evil spiritual warfare. I rest assured that You are making the pathway clear for me. Thank You for always being by my side, leading me through both still waters and trials. I know with You, Lord, I am on the winning side, Hallelujah! Amen!

My Reflection:

3. God's Word Is Healing

Verse:

- *1 Corinthians 6:14 (NIV):* "By his power God raised the Lord from the dead, and he will raise us also."

God's Whisper:

You are precious, My child. You are special in My sight. I love you! Let worship arise day and night, for I am holy; I love when you worship Me. Take off the shackles weighing you down. I have already cut them in two, but you need to release them. My power and might surround you now. Remember, as I have said in 1 Corinthians 6:14, I will raise you up like I have raised My son. I have the power to raise the dead. Stand firm in this knowledge! Your anxiety, worries, and problems are no match for Me. Give your burdens to Me. I can handle them. I am here to destroy your fear. When you worship, your singing not only lifts Me up but also lifts you up. If you stay close to My heart, I will show you great things. Please switch off the noise not from Me. Focus on Me, My words, My music. I will use My music to heal your soul. Remember to start each day with Me. I love you!

Personal:

In the early 1900s, revivalist Smith Wigglesworth had a powerful healing ministry in the United States and around the world. A story from one of his devotionals spoke about a very sick mom and daughter he encountered while traveling. He said to them, "Look, I've something in this bag that will cure every case in the world. It has never been known to fail." He shared more details on the remedy until they finally asked for a dose. He took out his Bible and read, "I am the Lord who heals you" (Exodus 15:26, NKJV). After he shared more wisdom on the power of God, both women claimed faith in God and were healed immediately.[4]

What an incredible story showing the amazing power in the mighty name of Jesus and the power of the Bible. Realize there is power in your voice speaking words of truth found in the Bible. There is also power in your voice when you worship and praise God. Choose your words wisely, praise the Lord often, and practice speaking God's word aloud today.

Suggested Worship:

"I Speak Jesus" by Charity Gayle featuring Steven Musso

Activation:

There is power in your voice! Believe God for healing today as Mr. Wigglesworth's did. Proclaim "I AM HEALED." Continue to praise God, believing He is healing you, by replaying today's suggested worship song.

Prayer: Jesus, I believe in Your mighty powerful name and Your word written in the Bible. I believe You are the Great Healer and have come to conquer death. I am so honored to be able to say Your name, Jesus. Your name is power over my life and my family, I thank and praise You today for loving me. Amen.

---

[4] Wigglesworth, Smith. *Smith Wigglesworth Devotional*. Whitaker House, 1999, pp 111.

My Reflection:

4. God Is a Warrior

Verses:

- *Exodus 15:2-3 (NIV):* "The Lord is my strength and my defense; he has become my salvation. He is my God, and I will praise him, my father's God, and I will exalt him. The Lord is a warrior; the Lord is his name."

God's Whisper:

I am here to fight for you, My child. I will fight for you as you sleep and when you wake. I will fight for you always to break down lies and strongholds around you. Sing to Me, reach out for Me, and I will rise up and fight for you. I am right here by your side. My strength will help you stand up and give you courage to face another day. I cover you today in My grace, mercy, and strength.

Personal:

Exodus chapter 14 is about the Red Sea moment where Pharoah's army was going after the Israelites, who were fleeing from Egypt's four-hundred-plus-year rule over them. The Lord was with the Israelites, who had been faithful to listen to the Lord. Once the Israelites safely crossed the Red Sea, the Lord eliminated Pharoah's army swiftly. What a mighty warrior! In Exodus 15, we find the Israelites praising God for fighting for them and saving each and every person.

I encourage you to get in your battle positions by singing and praising God as the warrior who will fight for you. He can defeat any enemy! Remember to always give praise to God. Don't grumble, but sing praises, always!

Suggested Worship:

"The Lord Is a Warrior" by Matt Papa featuring Shai Linne

Activation:

Shout out three times "Lord, You are my warrior!!!"

> **Prayer**: Lord, thank You for being My warrior. I get tired and frustrated sometimes, but today I am calling on You to stand in the gap for me and fight for me. I long to rest in Your arms and give You all my worries. Thank You, Lord, for hearing my prayer. Amen.

My Reflection:

5. God Is a Mighty Deliverer

Verses:

- *2 Samuel 22:2-3 (NIV):* "He said: 'The Lord is my rock, my fortress, and my deliverer; my God is my rock, in whom I take refuge, my shield and the horn of my salvation. He is my stronghold, my refuge, and my savior— from violent people you save me.'"

God's Whisper:

I am here to comfort you in every battle. I am beside you today as I was with Shadrach, Meshach, and Abednego in the fire. Call to Me now, I will deliver you! Remember I am living inside you and give you strength to face disappointment, fear, and anxiety. I come alongside you in your battles, I will never leave you alone. You are My first love.

Personal:

In the Bible, we see numerous amazing examples of God's delivering power. Today I will highlight two stories where God provided deliverance.

The first example is found in the Old Testament book of Daniel which describes Daniel and his three friends, Shadrach, Meshach, and Abednego. The first three chapters detail two deliverances. The first is when the boys were exiled to Babylon from Jerusalem. These young men were pressured to give up their Jewish identity, but they refused and remained faithful to the Torah (Hebrew Bible). God not only delivered them but elevated these boys to be servants in the royal palace. In chapter three, we learn Daniel's friends refused to bow down and worship the statue representing the Babylonian king and his kingdom. Due to disobedience to the king's orders, the three boys were punished and sentenced to be thrown in the fiery furnace. The fire was so hot it killed the soldiers who were walking the boys to the furnace! The king then said, "Look! I see four men walking around in the fire, unbound and unharmed, and the fourth looks like a son of the gods." The fourth man is believed to be Jesus. The king then came over and called the boys out of the fire. God delivered the boys once again and the king exalted them and acknowledged God as the true God.

The second example is found in Matthew 9:20-22 where we learn of a woman who was bleeding for twelve years, making her unclean and outcast. The woman had great faith as she pushed her way through the crowd, most likely crawling, and came up behind Jesus. She simply touched the edge of His cloak, and immediately her bleeding stopped. Jesus said "Your faith has healed you."

Notice in both examples the people had to go through great trials. The boys had threats of death, but they still were faithful; while the woman suffered for twelve years. Characters in both stories showed faith in the Lord. They believed in God's goodness, and God found favor with them and delivered them! Stand strong today in the Lord, believe He is your Deliverer. He is near to you and wants to deliver you.

Suggested Worship:

"Not My Battle" by Roma Waterman

Activation:

Be strong in the Lord today and shout, "I am a child of the One True God. I am Delivered."

Prayer: Lord, thank You that You are with me in all my struggles on this earth. I stand in Your strength today! May I live and act victorious over my struggles for I know You are with me. You have won the battle for me. I am delivered from my trials because of You. Amen!

My Reflection:

6. God Is Your Advocate, Your Helper

KRISTIN KURTZ

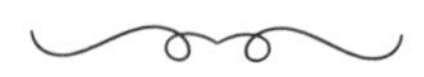

Verse:

- *John 15:26 (AMP):* "But when the Helper (Comforter, Advocate, Intercessor—Counselor, Strengthener, Standby) comes, whom I will send to you from the Father, *that is* the Spirit of Truth who comes from the Father, He will testify *and* bear witness about Me."

God's Whisper:

Look up My child. I am here for you. I am here with you. I will never leave you, not ever! I have been with you since the beginning. I created you to be special, to be My chosen child in this exact place, in this time in history. Let Me help you, guide you, let Me be your very best advocate in everything you do today. Remember I love you deeply.

Personal:

I was saved from addiction at age 25. I didn't have a true helper before that time. My help came from the next hit or drink to drown my sorrows and escape from the pain of the past. Only, as I found out, it made things worse. Now I am on the other side, and I know deep in my heart my help comes from the Lord. Sure, we can get help from family and friends, but at the end of the day, He will never leave. He is always there. Beloved, lean on Him. Get in the Word of God every day, before the noise of the world creeps in, so that He can be your Counselor.

Suggested Worship:

"Glory" by Jervis Campbell

Activation:

You are never far from the Lord, our Helper. The Holy Spirit is ALL-WAYS available. Lean in. Be still. The Holy Spirit is your strength and guide. ASK for HELP!

Prayer: Lord, I come to You with heavy weights—help me to lay them at the foot of the cross, daily. Throughout the day remind me how You are always there. Help me see You in the details, even in the trials and tribulations. Amen!

My Reflection:

7. Victory Is the Lord's

Verse:

- *Romans 8:37 (TPT):* "Yet even in the midst of all these things, we triumph over them all, for God has made us to be more than conquerors, and his demonstrated love is our glorious victory over everything!"

God's Whisper:

Victory is mine! I am here for you. Call to Me! I want to partner with you for your victory. Pray victorious prayers, not pleading prayers. You are a strong warrior in Me, so have the confidence to act like a mighty warrior. Stay grounded in My word, go forth, and pray My word today.

Personal:

In 1 Corinthians 15:57, we learn that Jesus' death gave us complete victory. This means we have victory from our struggles, sickness, and enemies. Because of His great love for us, Jesus said in Matthew 7:7-8 (NKJV), "Ask, and it will be given to you; seek, and you will find; knock, and it will be opened to you. For everyone who asks receives, and he who seeks finds, and to him who knocks it will be opened."

Prayer is powerful, especially when you are fighting on your knees before the Lord. This means prayer to Jesus can give you victory. Victory doesn't mean your struggles will be easy, but in obedience and prayer, victory can be found. English Theologian John Wesley said, "God does nothing except in response to believing prayer."[5] Romans 8:34 says Jesus is continually praying

---

[5] "John Wesley's Prayers." *The Spiritual Life*, https://slife.org/john-wesleys-prayers/. Accessed 6 April 2022.

for our triumph. Join Jesus in prayer over your life and pray from a place of victory.

Is there an area in your life you've been praying over? Perhaps an area you gave up praying for, feeling God forgot about you and isn't listening to you? Rest assured, God hasn't forgotten you. Pick up your prayers today. God loves you and wants to hear from you. Set aside time to pray and worship God, for He is good. Pray for specifics. God is omnipotent and knows the details, but He loves to hear it from you. Pray God will fight for you and that His will be done in your life. Seek the Lord to guide you in how to receive victory. Knock, and you will find new doors open from the Lord.

Suggested Worship:

"Battle Belongs" by Phil Wickham

Activation:

Follow the command found in Matthew 7:7-8 to ask, seek, and knock. Ask the Lord for victory for your trials today—remember, He has already won the war! Write down your prayer requests along with the date in the back of this book. In the future, go back and write down when those prayers are answered. Be prepared to be amazed at how His hand moves. Always be thankful for His work in your life.

Prayer: Dear Jesus, thank You for dying for my sins to set me free. I am asking today for Your victory in my struggles. I know I have victory in You and with You! I am seeking Your guidance for me in each step I take today, this week, and this month. I am knocking and asking You to open the perfect door for me to walk through today. Thank You for Your blood, Jesus, that covers me and the victory You have won for me. Amen!

My Reflection:

WEEK FOUR

God Provides for You

And my God shall supply
all your need according to His riches
in glory by Christ Jesus.

Philippians 4:19 (NKJV)

1. The Lord Will Provide

Verse:

- *Genesis 22:14 (NIV):* "So Abraham called that place The Lord Will Provide. And to this day it is said, 'On the mountain of the Lord it will be provided.'"

God's Whisper:

My child, when you think of provision, don't only think of wealth. I have provided for you the birds of the air, the flowers in the field, and the blue sky to admire and enjoy. I am always thinking of you and want to bless you in more ways than you can imagine. My child, trust Me to provide your needs. I love you and long to give you your heart's desire. Open your eyes to the wonders I have created around you. Seek Me now and know that I am your Great Provider.

Personal:

My friend Kristin suggested I read a book called *Gift of the Red Bird: The Story of a Divine Encounter* by Paula D'Arcy.[6] In this book, D'Arcy stepped out of her comfort zone and journeyed solo into the wilderness for three days to get closer to God. She longed to learn God's mysteries by listening to Him in the quiet of the woods. This book opened my eyes to learning how to see and hear God everywhere. Although I knew God was everywhere, I didn't pay close attention to details around me until after reading this book. Now I try to get outside daily unless it's cold and windy! I particularly like walking in nature, hearing the birds sing or snow crunch under my feet. I love seeing

---

[6] D'Arcy, Paula. *The Gift of the Red Bird: A Spiritual Encounter: with a Guide for Reflection*. Crossroad Publishing Co, 1996.

all God has created for me to enjoy. His provision of beauty in nature amazes me daily.

On my walks last year, I started bringing a notebook to write down fun and interesting things that the Lord showed me. I have been amazed by how God uses rocks, water, flowers and all sorts of animals to speak to me. I've discovered that the Lord gives me more insights when I am alone and not distracted by chatting with friends. I find it helpful to be purposeful and focus on Him, not on burning calories.

One occasion while I was out for a walk along the beautiful Lake Superior, I was searching for a flat rock to skip across the surface of the lake. Although the shore was strewn with rocks, I couldn't find any flat rocks until the Lord opened my eyes and I found the perfect rock wedged into a very large boulder. When I went to grab the rock, I found it was stuck at two points. I had to work hard to get the first barrier removed, and then the second barrier rock was easier to remove. As I sat and pondered this experience, I heard the Lord say this rock represented victory from the struggles I was going through. I kept that rock as a reminder of my experience and a reminder of the victory I have in Christ and that God will always provide.

Suggested Worship:

"If Jireh by Elevation Worship was a Piano Solo" by YoungMin You

Activation:

Spend additional time with the Lord today and soak in worship music of your choice. Take note of all the beauty He has provided for you. The best way is to go on a walk, preferably outside to be surrounded by nature.

Prayer: Here I am, Lord. I lift my life up to You now. I worship You and thank You for all You have provided and will provide for me. Thank you for the flowers, the trees and the birds. How awesome Lord is Your creation. Amen!

My Reflection:

2. God Is the Multiplier

Verses:

- *Matthew 14:14-16 (NIV)*: "When Jesus landed and saw a large crowd, he had compassion on them and healed their sick. As evening approached, the disciples came to him and said, 'This is a remote place, and it's already getting late. Send the crowds away, so they can go to the villages and buy themselves some food.' Jesus replied, 'They do not need to go away. You give them something to eat.'

God's Whisper:

I, the Lord your God, am a multiplier and seek to multiply treasures for you. Treasures you will find not only in food, clothing, or other provisions but also in beauty around you. Look for Me and what I do for your life. I long to multiply My glory for you every day. Reach out and ask Me. I long to give you more than you could imagine.

Personal:

The story of Jesus feeding the five thousand with simply five loaves and two fish described in Matthew 14 was only one of the miracles that day. Did you notice Jesus healed many first and then miraculously fed them? I hadn't noticed until recently. I also found it interesting Jesus told the disciples to give the crowds something to eat. Jesus challenged His disciples, who had just witnessed healings, to feed a large crowd and not send them to town to purchase food. Although Jesus had the power to feed the people on His own, as He did when He turned water into wine, He wanted to empower the disciples to act by providing direction for them. Jesus used both a little boy's sacrifice of his lunch and His disciple's obedience to complete the great miracle. This story continues by showing how everyone had their fill of food with an abundance of twelve baskets of food left over.

Don't underestimate what God can do in your life. He is the God of miracles and He loves to greatly exceed your expectations in fun and creative ways. Trust God's plans are perfect and allow Him to use the skills He uniquely gave you. Believe God will work through you, and ensure you are ready to move when God says to move. Remember Jesus is the same yesterday, today, and forever, and He wants to use each of us to be a vessel for miracles both big and small here on earth.

Suggested Worship:

"The Blessing" featuring Kari Jobe & Cody Carnes, Elevation Worship

Activation:

Grab two glasses and fill one with water. Set a timer for five minutes, carefully pour one drop of water to the empty glass for each blessing from God in your life. Push out negative, self-pitying thoughts and turn them into positive ones. If your coffee is cold, thank God you have coffee; if your phone is old, thank God you have a phone. Notice how quickly blessings multiply in your glass. Afterward, thank the Lord for all He has done in your life, big and small. Finally, drink your glass of "blessing" water.

Prayer: Lord, I am forever grateful for Your kindness and the bountiful gifts You provide me. Open my eyes to see Your goodness and blessings surrounding me. Please use me today to bless others. Amen!

My Reflection:

3. *God Is More than Enough*

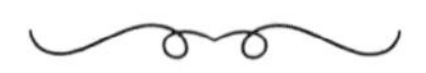

Verse:

- *Psalm 46:1 (TPT):* "God, you're such a safe and powerful place to find refuge! You're a proven help in time of trouble—*more than enough* and always available whenever I need you."

God's Whisper:

My child, come running to Me. I will provide you safety from fears, trials, and enemies. I am here with My arms stretched out for you. Come to Me, come now quickly. Enjoy My safety and comfort. Feel My love for you today. Let Me help you. I am always here for you. Call on Me, and I will show you I am more than enough.

Personal:

In Psalm 46, the writer describes calling out to God in his time of trouble. I like how The Message translation of Psalm 46 provides bold examples of what trouble could look like: "We stand fearless at the cliff-edge of doom, courageous in seastorm and earthquake, before the rush and roar of oceans, the tremors that shift mountains. Jacob-wrestling God fights for us, God-of-Angel-Armies protects us." Wow! Fearless at the cliff-edge of doom is powerful imagery of God's strength that is more than enough for us. Be encouraged to remember God is always present to help you. This means when you are weak and in trouble, God is strong for you. God is your refuge, your protection in any moment of distress, sadness, or worry.

I am thankful my earthly troubles are nothing compared to

what the writer of Psalm 46 faced many years ago. Nevertheless, I found myself in despair for many years over a relationship I valued. I felt trapped and that I had no voice. It was hard for me to call on God then. At the peak of my despair, I found it hard to read the Bible or even pray for many months. God felt distant to me. Finally, I decided to pick up my Bible and call out to the Lord for help and strength. Little by little, my confidence and strength came back, and I was refreshed and strengthened by the Lord. I found my voice again! I believe I am a stronger advocate for others due to my trials. I now know in the future when I am in the middle of a trial I need to take time to be alone with God. I need to play worship music and praise Him, especially when I don't feel like it. I know God will make me stronger. He is more than enough.

Suggested Worship:

"More Than Enough" by Jesus Culture, featuring Kim Walker-Smith

Activation:

Sit and imagine a stone fountain overflowing with water. Now imagine you are the fountain and the Lord is the water. Imagine His love, strength, and protection pouring over you right now. Pause and rest in that comforting image for one minute.

Prayer: Thank You, Father, for your overflowing strength and protection over me. Thank You for never giving up on me and always being available to me. Thank You for being more than enough for me, more than enough for my trials, fears, and enemies. I give you all my unwanted trials because I know You can handle them. I believe for more with You today; more peace, more love, more joy. Amen!

My Reflection:

4. Life Giver, Blessing Giver

Verses:

- *Job 10:12 (NIV):* "You gave me life and showed me kindness, and in your providence watched over my spirit."
- *John 10:10 (TPT):* "A thief has only one thing in mind—he wants to steal, slaughter, and destroy. But I have come to *give you everything in abundance, more than you expect*—life in its fullness until you overflow!

God's Whisper:

My dear precious child, I am the source of all life. I chose to create you from the beginning of time. You are so special to Me, My child. I not only gave you this earthly life, but I want to give you life abundantly now and for eternity. Simply trust in Me. I cherish the time you spend with Me. Let Me revive your soul today.

Personal:

The book of Job in the Bible tells us of a man who greatly loved and feared God. Job thanked God even when his life was falling apart. He thanked God even though his possessions were destroyed, his children died, and he developed painful sores all over his body. Amid his great sorrow, he did not sin or curse God, but instead, Job thanked God for his life, for showing him kindness, and for watching over him. Years later God blessed Job greatly with wealth, health, and family due to Job's faith. In fact, Job 42:10 (NIV) states, "After Job had prayed for his friends, the Lord restored his fortunes and gave him twice as much as he had before."

Just like the example of Job's life, the enemy always sets out to steal, kill, and destroy, but God has come to give life abundantly. Pastor David Guzik said, "Abundant life doesn't mean it is an especially long life. Abundant life isn't an easy, comfortable life. Abundant life is a life of satisfaction and contentment in Jesus."[7] Look to Jesus. He is the life giver, blessing giver. Lean on Him for joy everlasting. Be encouraged today with God's blessings.

Suggested Worship:

"Life Giver" by Ark Creative

Activation:

Thankfulness blesses the Lord, so spend time today and thank the Lord for His blessings. Grab a pen and write down five things for which you are thankful.

1.____

2.____

3.____

4.____

5.____

Prayer: Thank You, Lord, for the many blessings You have given me. May I use every moment to glorify You and honor You today. Teach me to be ever thankful for all You have provided for me. Everything You speak in your Word is like a joyous treasure. I receive Your gift of reviving me afresh today. Amen.

---

[7] "John 10—The Good Shepherd." Enduring Word, https://enduringword.com/bible-commentary/john-10/. Used with permission © 2022 The Enduring Word Bible Commentary by David Guzik—ewm@enduringword.com.

My Reflection:

5. God of Creation

Verses:

- *Psalms 77:13-14 (TPT):* "It's here in your presence, in your sanctuary, where I learn more of your ways, for holiness is revealed in everything you do. Lord, you're the one and only, the great and glorious God! Your display of wonders, miracles, and power makes the nations acknowledge you."
- *John 1:1-3 (NIV):* "In the beginning was the Word, and the Word was with God, and the Word was God. He was with God in the beginning. Through him all things were made; without him nothing was made that has been made."

God's Whisper:

My child, thank you for spending time with Me today. I want to speak to your heart and tell you great and marvelous things about you, and about the world around you. I am doing great miracles even now because miracles are not only for the days of old. Look for Me in the stars, the sunrise, and on a moonlit night. I have created these wonders for you, with you in mind. I am always thinking about you, My child.

Personal:

I love to travel, whether it's an hour away to hike a new trail or a five-hour flight across the country to visit mountains and oceans. There are so many miles of vast and varied beauty to explore in our world. I prefer quiet places to enjoy God's creation and be surrounded by nature. I especially like watching a sunrise or sunset. No matter where I am, I stop and marvel at the wonders God created. God is good and created so much variety on this earth to appreciate and admire. I pray you are able to experience some of the beauty near you. I encourage you to stop today and look for divine appointments from God to see His wonders, whether in the beauty of nature or in your friends around you.

Psalm 77 reminds me of a time I was in Alaska. When I turned a corner, my breath was taken away because in front of me was a wide expanse of snow-capped mountains. I found the closer I drove to the mountain range, the more spectacular the beauty. I encourage you to go deeper and further with God. Be expectant and excited for what God has waiting for you in His creation.

Suggested Worship:

"Sanctuary" by River Valley Worship

Activation:

Grab a pencil, pen, or crayons and draw a picture of one of the wonders of God's creation. The sky's the limit: the mountains, the ocean, animals big or small, flowers, anything. Enjoy this creative time with God.

Prayer: Lord, thank You for creating this beautiful world to admire and enjoy. Help me to stop and see more of Your beauty today. I appreciate the details of Your creation. Open my eyes to Your miracles and power around me today. Amen!

My Reflection:

6. Bloom with God

Verses:

- *Matthew 13:37 (NLT):* "Jesus replied, 'The Son of Man is the farmer who plants the good seed.'"
- *Psalms 92:12-13 (NLT):* "But the godly will flourish like palm trees and grow strong like the cedars of Lebanon. For they are transplanted to the Lord's own house. They flourish in the courts of our God."

God's Whisper:

My dear sweet child, I am here to prune what needs to be removed from your life. I am here to set you free from what is not from me and is stealing your strength. Let Me work in you. My hand's work will only make you lighter. Let Me transplant you from your past. I have great plans for you. You need to only look forward in this life with Me. Blossoms are blooming everywhere in Your future with Me.

Personal:

I don't have a particularly green thumb, but I still like to dabble with growing a few herbs and vegetables. This past year I tried growing microgreens in a tiny indoor greenhouse. I was surprised to learn many microgreens can grow to maturity in six to eight days compared to about thirty to fifty days for a regular vegetable. These microgreens, which look like tiny sprouts, are packed full of nutrients and are perfect to add to a salad or sandwich. Some sources said one serving of a microgreen provides thirty times the nutrients of a full serving of the respective vegetable. Isn't that incredible? Fast-growing and full of nutrients! The Lord highlighted for me that in this decade, this new season for the United States, believers need to grow quickly and deeply with the Lord by spending dedicated time with Jesus and remaining rooted in Him. When we do this, Jesus can create an amazingly rich understanding of Him. In addition, the fruits can multiply quickly and produce a bountiful harvest. Along the way, you will grow in beautiful spiritual maturity.

The Lord cares so tenderly for you that sometimes He lovingly prunes away what you have in your life that is harmful, sometimes including things you didn't realize were harmful. John 15:2 (TPT) states, "He cares for the branches connected to me by lifting and propping up the fruitless branches and pruning every fruitful branch to yield a greater harvest." Ask the Lord what you need to have pruned today so you can grow deeper in Him. Once you are pruned, you have the ability to quickly grow stronger in the Lord.

Suggested Worship:

"The Garden" by Kari Jobe

Activation:

Pause a moment, take a deep breath, and smell some fresh flowers, fresh fruit, or fresh vegetables. Pause to reflect how the item grows with sun, light, and soil. Thank God for the variety He has created for you to enjoy.

Prayer: Thank You Lord for working in me and pruning what is not meant to be in my life. I know You prune me because of Your pure love for me. Let my roots quickly grow deep in You, for I know in You I will have freedom. Precious Lord Jesus, pour Your love over me now. Amen!

My Reflection:

7. Supplier of Your Needs

Verse:

- *Philippians 4:19 (NKJV):* "And my God shall supply all your need according to His riches in glory by Christ Jesus."

God's Whisper:

My child, I am with you always. I am your provider now and forevermore. I breathe on you afresh today. Sit and soak in My presence now. I have only goodness and mercy for you. Push away the enemy boldly with your prayers. Your words are more powerful than you know. Cling to Me now. I want to share with you how I want to provide for each and every need. Come to me and discover My ways are higher than your ways. Get to know My will for you. I want to give you the desires of your heart. I love you, My child.

Personal:

The Bible says the Lord will supply every need according to His riches in glory in Christ Jesus. Notice, God does not say He would provide all your wants. Examples of needs include food, shelter, and clothing while examples of wants could include dining out, an extravagant home, or name brand clothing.

An impressive example in the Bible of the Lord providing needs is found in Psalm 78:24-25 when the Lord provided the Israelites with manna: "He rained down on them manna to eat and gave them the grain from heaven. Man ate the bread of angels; he sent them food in abundance" (ESV). First, we see an incredible miracle that happened for the Israelites; they received bread known as manna from heaven. Manna is described as wafer-type bread with the flavor of honey which had to be baked or boiled before they ate it. We know they needed to go and gather the manna each morning and cook it, except on their Sabbath. Next, we see the bread was that of angels; it was truly heavenly bread. Imagine how delicious it must have been! Finally, we note that the Lord sent the manna to them in abundance, meaning way more than they needed was provided. Why did God supply so much? It is because they put their trust in God.

Did you notice that while God provided the manna, the Israelites still had to get up and go gather the food and cook it? They could not just sit and be served; they had to move. Take great comfort in the Lord's provision, and ask the Lord what He has already provided you that you need to get up and go after. I encourage you today not to be anxious about anything. In Jeremiah 29:11 (NLT), the Lord says, "For I know the plans I have for you . . . They are plans for good and not for disaster, to give you a future and a hope." Trust that everything you need will be made available for you to gather like manna.

Suggested Worship:

"More than Enough" by Micah Dillon

Activation:

Speak the following words of declaration to the Lord: "Lord, You are my Provider for all my needs. Please Lord, take away the desires for my wants that are not from You."

Prayer: Thank You, Lord, for being my great Provider. Let my faith not grow weak, but help me remember Your will for my life is good. Please show me what You have provided for me that I need to steward today. Help me to rest in the knowledge that You have great plans for me to succeed and prosper in Your good will. Amen!

My Reflection:

WEEK FIVE

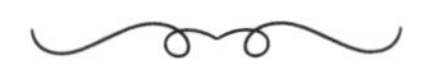

God Chose You

But even before I was born,
God chose me and called me by his
marvelous grace.

Galatians 1:15a (NLT)

1. You Are Chosen to Release God's Breath

KRYSTAL RASMUSSEN

Verses:

- *Acts 2:2-4 (ESV):* "And suddenly there came from heaven a sound like a mighty rushing wind, and it filled the entire house where they were sitting. And divided tongues as of fire appeared to them and rested on each one of them. And they were all filled with the Holy Spirit and began to speak in other tongues as the Spirit gave them utterance."

God's Whisper:

My precious child, let Me breathe on you afresh again today. Let My breath stir up the fires I've placed inside you. Watch My breath strengthen you, embolden you, and cause you to come alive even more in Me. Just like the wind, My breath is not meant to be harnessed but released. My living breath will cause you to flow in a beautiful dance with Me that will affect the world around you. Release My breath, and let's create My Kingdom on earth together.

Personal:

The wind and breath of God changes you—or perhaps a better way to state this, it awakens you to who you were created to be. There are so many beautiful accounts in Scripture of the wind and breath of God. Feats include creating life as it was exhaled into Adam, empowering Samson as it came upon him for victory, causing dry bones to come alive, and perhaps most notable, coming like a mighty rushing wind and ushering in tongues of fire. You see the breath of life produces something both in the spirit and in the natural. So when the wind and breath of God come upon you, partner with it! Speak, prophesy, preach, pray in unknown tongues, and watch because you just joined what the Father in heaven is wanting to do in the earth, and His word never returns void. Yes, you are anointed and chosen to receive and release the wind and breath of God.

Suggested Worship:

"Flame of Fire, Rushing Wind" by Bryan & Katie Torwalt

Activation:

Today, believe you are anointed to receive and release the wind and breath of God. Boldly say, "I AM ANOINTED!" until your spirit is burning as the breath of God ignites the fires deep within you. Speak this over yourself several times. Speak it with a little bit of attitude because you know who you are and you are proud to be a child of the one true God! Declare over yourself, "I receive and release the wind and breath of God!" You need to get this deep inside of you because the time is now that the Lord is going to pour out so much upon you.

Prayer: Father, thank You for breathing upon me afresh by Your Holy Spirit. Show me today how You want me to release Your wind and breath. I pray that when I release Your wind and breath it's like a mighty lion's roar that makes heaven rejoice and hell tremble. Let it create a sound that draws people's spirit like in Acts 2:6 because they are being drawn to You. I choose to always partner with Your wind and breath, and I pray they create an exhilarating life dance between You and me all the days of my life. Amen!

My Reflection:

2. God Chose You to Be Holy

Verse:

- *Leviticus 11:44a (NIV):* "I am the Lord your God; consecrate yourselves and be holy, because I am holy."

God's Whisper:

I ask you today, My child, to ask for forgiveness and consecrate yourself before Me. In doing so, you will be able to hear Me speak to you clearly. There won't be any barriers between you and Me. I love you, and I want to show you greater things for you on this earth. I am a just ruler, patient and kind. Thank you for your heart to spend time with Me. I will honor this time and bless you.

Personal:

In Leviticus 11 we learn God asks us to consecrate ourselves and be holy because He is holy. You may ask, what is consecration? According to King James Dictionary,the word *consecrate*[8] means to set apart or separate. Kathryn Kuhlman, an evangelist, said there is closeness when you follow the Holy Spirit. She said, surrender your will to the will of God, and then the two will become one. She said the Holy Spirit intercedes boldly for you before the throne of God and prays with you, through you, and in you.[9] One way to be closer to the Father, Son, and Holy Spirit

---

[8] "Consecrate." *Bible Study Tools*, https://www.biblestudytools.com/dictionaries/king-james-dictionary/consecrate.html. Accessed 29 March 2022.

[9] Kathryn Kuhlman, "The Importance of Consecration & Communion with the Spirit." YouTube, uploaded by Prophetic News Now 15 April 2021, https://www.youtube.com/watch?v=le3vN8fePXQ.

is to have communion (see today's Activation). Communion is an act of obedience, a time for remembering Jesus' sacrificial death on the cross for us.

Suggested Worship:

"Holy, Holy, Holy (We Bow Before Thee)" by Shane & Shane

Additional Worship:

"Nothing but the Blood, O the Blood of Jesus" by Sarah Hart Pearsons

Activation:

After listening to one of today's song selections, take time to have communion with God. First, if you haven't asked Jesus to be your Lord and Savior, look at page ten and ask Jesus into your life. Before communion, ask the Lord to reveal any unconfessed sin, pride, or negative thoughts. Next, get ready to set up your communion. You can use whatever you have on hand for the elements: a cracker, chip, or piece of bread; juice, wine, or water. Feel free to grab a friend or family member, or do communion by yourself. Now read the following aloud:

> Lord, as I take the bread representing Your body that was broken for me, I remember You and thank You for Your faithfulness and love for me. You took the awful punishment for me when You died for me—thank You! Thank You that Your death gave me abundant and eternal life. Today, I receive this bread in remembrance of You. (You may now eat your bread.)
>
> In the same way, I take this cup representing Your blood poured out for me. Because of Your great sacrifice and blood shed for me, I can be free from the penalty of sin. Thank You for Your great sacrifice for me. Today I remember You and thank You for this blood shed for me. (You may now drink your beverage.)

Prayer: Thank You, Jesus, for the power of Your blood. Thank You for reminding me of the importance of consecrating myself through the act of communion. May I live today boldly for You and proclaim You are Lord. Amen!

My Reflection:

3. *You Were Designed to Worship*

Verses:

- *John 4:23 (NIV):* "Yet a time is coming and has now come when the true worshipers will worship the Father in the Spirit and in truth, for they are the kind of worshipers the Father seeks."
- *Psalm 150:6 (NIV):* "Let everything that has breath praise the Lord. Praise the Lord."

God's Whisper:

My dear child, I covet your worship. Give Me praise today. I long to hear your voice singing praises to Me. When you sing, I hear your worship from heaven on high. Your song reverberates through the heavens, and the angels rejoice. Your praise and worship are powerful and lovely. Your worship will bring you higher to be with Me today.

Personal:

Today is a good day—a glorious day—because our Savior made today. As Psalm 118:24 says, "This is the day the Lord has made; We will rejoice and be glad in it" (NKJV). Rejoice today, my friend! Before you get distracted by your day, thank the Lord, for He made today just for you. Start your day with one or two worship songs to set your focus on the Lord and praise God for a new day He has made. Worshiping God lifts Him up, and He loves to hear our praises. Psalm 100:4 (NIV) states, "Enter his gates with thanksgiving and his courts with praise; give thanks to him and praise his name."

Theologian A.W. Tozer said, "Worship is man's full reason for existence. Worship is why we are born and why we are born again."[10] The Bible has numerous references in the Old and New Testaments stating we should worship God, our King of Kings. God requests worship, but it is important to have a tender heart while we worship and not do so grudgingly or to make a false pretense and be showy like the Pharisees in the Bible.

I have known people who skip the worship section of their weekend church service because the music is not their style, is too loud, or doesn't feel valuable to them. If I just described you, I encourage you to attend worship this week. Go to church early, and be ready to worship; maybe find headphones or earplugs to decrease the noise level. Engage in the worship and watch what God will do!

Suggested Worship:

"Crown Him" by I AM THEY

Activation:

Do you play an instrument? If so, even if it has been a long time, go and play your instrument again today. Make a joyful noise to the Lord (Psalm 100:1, ESV). If you don't have an instrument, sing or hum a hymn you know well.

Prayer: Lord, I lift Your name on high. I crown You today, for today is the day You have made. Thank You for Your majesty and wonder. May I praise Your name and worship You throughout the day today, for You are worthy of all my praise. Amen!

---

[10] Tozer, A.W., Snyder, James. *The Purpose of Man: Designed to Worship*. Bethany House, 2009, back cover.

My Reflection:

4. God Chose You to Sit at His Table

Verses:

- *Song of Songs 2:4 (NIV):* "Let him lead me to the banquet hall, and let his banner over me be love."
- *Psalm 60:4 (ESV):* "You have set up a banner for those who fear you, that they may flee to it from the bow. Selah."

God's Whisper:

My banner over you is love. I, the Lord your God, created you, and I rule over all creation. My love for you is great. Pour out your love for Me, and I will cover you with My presence. Rest in Me, for I am love. I cover you with love always. Believe and receive My love. Look up and see My glory surrounding you now. Feel My presence always. I am never far. I am always close to you, My child. Feel My wraparound presence and My embrace.

Personal:

In Doug Addison's book "Hearing God Every Day,"[11] he talks about a vision he had of a long table in heaven. Seated at the table was God and only a few other people. They were enjoying His presence, but there were many empty chairs. Addison also saw numerous butlers and servants standing at attention, waiting for orders from the King. Although these servants were sincere and wanted to serve God, they were unaware God wanted them to come to the table and get to know Him personally.

---

[11] Addison, Doug. "Discovering How God Speaks." *Hearing God Every Day*. Destiny Image® Publishing Inc, 2019, pp. 13.

Can you imagine sitting at the Lord's banquet table? What would you say to Him? What questions would you ask? What exciting things of your day would you want to share with Him? Although you aren't physically sitting at His table now, realize in the spiritual realm you can be. Don't be distracted by the busyness of serving God, but instead take time to get to know God more! Go ahead and share your heart with the Lord today and be willing to sit and ask Him what is on His heart to share with you. Once I started to ask God what was on His heart, He was thrilled I asked, and He shared His beautiful thoughts with me.

Suggested Worship and Activation:

When I was a child, I learned sign language for a song titled "His Banner Over Me is Love." I encourage you to find a video to learn sign language for this song. Please watch and do the motions along with this video. This is powerful and activates your body, mind, and spirit.

Prayer: Lord, I thank You for Your great love for me and Your banner of love always present and surrounding me. May I always give You honor, praise, and thanks for Your love. May I get to know Your heart for me more today as I sit in Your presence. Amen!

My Reflection:

5. God Designed You for His Glory

Verse:

- *Psalm 3:3 (TPT):* "But *in the depths of my heart I truly know* that you, Yahweh, have become my Shield; You take me and surround me with yourself. Your glory covers me continually. You lift high my head."

God's Whisper:

I am here now with you. Look up, My child. I am all around you. I move with you and go with you wherever you go. You don't have to look hard. Just ask Me, and I will show you My glory. When you look for Me and see Me, I am overjoyed. I want to share so much with you. Even in your darkest nights, I am there with you. Call out to Me, and I will answer. I am there for you. I laugh when you laugh, cry when you cry. I am there to be Your mighty warrior ready to battle in your most troubling nights. I love you, My child.

Personal:

Did you know we were created and designed for God's glory? We were born to live in His glory. You may ask what is glory? The glory of God is His weighty presence. You may feel His presence more when you worship God in a group or perhaps by yourself because worship can lead us deeper into glory. Pastor Bill Johnson has said there are several levels of glory and you can step up deeper with worship—every taste of good is an invitation for more.[12] It is important to remember God will not

---

[12] Bill Johnson, "What Is God's Glory?" YouTube, uploaded by Akinaa, 19 January 2019, https://www.youtube.com/watch?v=BK8u4MxdjH8.

inhabit an atmosphere that is not spiritually clean. To have a clean atmosphere, we must pray and ask for forgiveness. Romans 3:23 (NKJV) says, "for all have sinned and fall short of the glory of God," so we all have something to confess. Afterward, you can ask for God's peace and love to return to you. I encourage you not to hurry in the Lord's presence; pause, rest, focus on Him, and just be in His presence.

In order to get a glimpse of what God's presence looks like, let's read Ezekiel 1:27-28 (NIV), which says, "I saw that from what appeared to be his waist up he looked like glowing metal, as if full of fire, and that from there down he looked like fire; and brilliant light surrounded him. Like the appearance of a rainbow in the clouds on a rainy day, so was the radiance around him. This was the appearance of the likeness of the glory of the LORD. When I saw it, I fell facedown, and I heard the voice of one speaking." Can you imagine seeing the Lord like this?

Suggested Worship:

"Lord You Have My Heart (& Spontaneous Worship)" by Clare Bell

Activation:

Shout out to the Lord, "Show me Your glory today, Lord!" Next, take time to soak in God's glory. Sit or lie down, tune out all distractions, and enjoy the worship song again.

Prayer: Lord, open my eyes and show me Your glory. You are all I want. You are all I need. My mind can't comprehend how grand and glorious You are Lord. Thank You for continually covering me with Your glory. Amen!

My Reflection:

6. God's Glory Shines Through You

Verse:

- *Psalms 19:1 (NIV):* "The heavens declare the glory of God; the skies proclaim the work of his hands."

God's Whisper:

Dear child, even in times of trouble, I am with you. I am mightily working for you. Lift your voice in praise to Me. It blesses Me as much as it blesses you and your family. I am here for you. Lean on Me, and let Me show you My glory. Let it shine around you. My presence within you will glow and shine brightly to bring others to you because they will see Me in you. I humbly ask for your time. Seek a quiet space for a few minutes to listen to Me share special words just for you, My child.

Personal:

The book Habakkuk in the Old Testament contains three chapters documenting the prophet Habakkuk. Chapter three depicts Habakkuk's prayer during turbulent times when he knew difficult days were still to come. Yet Habakkuk gives God praise even with his heart pounding and lips quivering from fear. In verses 3b-4 (NIV) the prayer says, "His glory covered the heavens and his praise filled the earth. His splendor was like the sunrise; rays flashed from his hand, where his power was hidden." In verse 18, Habakkuk continues, "yet I will rejoice in the LORD, I will be joyful in God my Savior."

I believe we are now in times similar to Habakkuk's day where the Lord's full power is hidden from the world. However, through the praises of His people, His glory will pour over this land and heal those searching for healing. We need to focus on rejoicing in the Lord and use our collective worship to unleash our sound to give praise and honor to the Lord. It may not be easy some days, but be joyful and obedient in the process and think of Habakkuk. In doing so, you bless His holy name and His light will shine through you.

Suggested Worship:

"Healing Is Coming (Habakkuk's Prayer)" by Amanda Scrimale

Activation:

Sing the words or hum the tune to "This Little Light of Mine" to engage your voice. Let the Lord's light shine brightly through you.

Prayer: Lord, thank You for revealing to me the story of Habakkuk. I ask that You help me give You praise even when there are turbulent times around me. I thank and praise You, Lord, for who You are to me. I ask You to pour out Your glory on me so Your light can shine through me. I am in awe that You want to get to know me more. Let my actions be pure today and honor You. Amen!

My Reflection:

7. The Lord Chose You

KRYSTAL RASMUSSEN

Verses:

- *Ruth 3:13 (TPT):* "Stay here tonight, and I will protect you. In the morning, we'll see if he's willing to redeem you. If he does, good; let him. But if he refuses to redeem you, then I promise, as surely as Yahweh lives, I will. So sleep here until morning."
- *Ruth 4:6 (TPT):* "At this, the kinsman-redeemer balked and said, 'In that case, I'm not able to redeem it for myself without risking my inheritance. Take my purchase option of redemption yourself, for I can't do it.'"

God's Whisper:

My beloved, I am truly Your Redeemer. There is such a sweet rest for you when you see Me as such. Through My blood, you now share My kingdom inheritance. One look at you and I knew you were worth the risk. I would have risked everything just for you, My dear one. That is how precious you are to Me.

Personal:

When I think of Jesus as my Redeemer there is no better demonstration in Scripture than Boaz, who risked his inheritance to redeem Ruth. Was Ruth, a Moabite woman, worth the risk or worthy of redemption? Scripture clearly shows us she, as a direct ancestor of Jesus, truly was, and so are you. Your Redeemer, Jesus, says you are worthy—you were worth the cross. No matter what you've walked through in your past, Jesus says, "I chose you."

Suggested Worship:

"Rescue Story" by Zach Williams

Activation:

Today's activation is simple. Look up to heaven like you are looking into your beloved Jesus' eyes and say, "I chose You too." Adding "too" is significant. It will simultaneously do something in your mind and your heart. Then take a moment to pause in thankfulness for all that Your Redeemer has done for you.

Prayer: Father, I come before You knowing I am fully redeemed by Jesus. Thank You for choosing me from before the beginning of time to be Yours. I rest in the comfort and peace that Jesus is my Redeemer. I know no failure or success could ever alter the fact that I am redeemed by my beloved Jesus. Continue to highlight to me this day my precious Redeemer so I can continually pause to give Him great thanks. Amen!

My Reflection:

WEEK SIX

God's Peace For You

These things I have spoken to you,
that in Me you may have peace.
In the world you will have
tribulation; but be of good cheer,
I have overcome the world.

JOHN 16:33 (NKJV)

1. Your Hiding Place

Verses:

- *Psalm 32:7 (NIV):* "You are my hiding place; you will protect me from troubleand surround me with songs of deliverance."
- *Psalm 36:7 (TPT):* "O God, how extravagant is your cherishing love! All mankind can find a hiding place under the shadow of your wings."

God's Whisper:

I am the Lord, El Shaddai. Come to Me all who are weary and heavy-laden, and I will give you rest. Seek Me, and you will find Me today. I long to comfort you, renew and refresh you. I am here waiting for you. Your days may be long and full of turmoil, but call to Me and I will answer. I will rescue you and place you in My hiding place where no one and nothing will harm you.

Personal:

One of my favorite books is *The Hiding Place*. It tells the story of the ten Boom family who lived in Holland during World War II and hid Jews. Eventually, their family was forced into a concentration camp. I was in awe of how the ten Boom sisters stood on God's word and truth during this unimaginable experience. I cried when I read their story and learned of the miracles that happened to the sisters to keep them safe and was reminded God was with them. One of my favorite examples was when Corrie and her sister were able to hide a Bible and bring it into the concentration camp. This miracle allowed the girls to read to their bunkmates daily and provide encouragement, comfort, and great peace. Corrie ten Boom said in her book, "There are no 'ifs' in God's kingdom...His timing is perfect. His will is our hiding place. Lord Jesus, keep me in Your will! Don't let me go mad by poking about outside it."[13]

The ten Boom sisters were strong in their faith while in the concentration camp, in part, because they were grounded in the Bible from an early age. They each hid God's word in their heart during the good times so when the trials of war came they could rely on and rest in God's provision. God mightily used this imprisoned family for His purpose to give hope and be a light for the Lord. Corrie went on to spread God's light for many years after being released. This is the power of making God your hiding place.

Suggested Worship:

"You Are My Hiding Place" by Victoria Orenze (this video is twelve minutes long but well worth your time)

Activation:

Hide God's word in your heart today so in times of trouble you can rely on His word. I suggest you start by memorizing Psalm 32:7 listed above.

Prayer: Lord, in the storms, trials, and tribulations, I will trust in You. I know Your timing is perfect, Lord. Please give me patience and faith today. When I am weak, You are strong, Lord. You are my hiding place. Thank You, Lord, for hiding me under Your wings and giving me rest. Amen!

[13] ten Boom, Corrie, et al. *The Hiding Place*. 1971. Chosen Books, 1984, pp. 234.

My Reflection:

2. Eagle's Wings

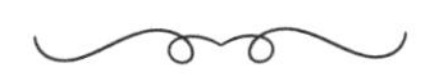

Verses:

- *Psalm 91:3-4 (NIV):* "Surely he will save you from the fowler's snare and from the deadly pestilence. He will cover you with his feathers, and under his wings you will find refuge; his faithfulness will be your shield and rampart."
- *Isaiah 40:30-31 (NIV):* "Even youths grow tired and weary, and young men stumble and fall; but those who hope in the LORD will renew their strength. They will soar on wings like eagles; they will run and not grow weary, they will walk and not be faint."

God's Whisper:

Watch Me soar above the storms, dear child. I don't get weighed down by the gossip or the drudgery of the world. I want you to come up higher with Me. I want you to fly high with Me. Join Me, and I will give you a new perspective. I will keep you safe above life's storms. You may experience some wrath and strong winds of the world, but when you soar with Me, you will feel peace, safety, and protection. Take heart, dear one, for I have overcome the world.

Personal:

Did you ever notice how graceful and regal eagles are? They soar high above the earth with ease. It is said that eagles sense when storms are coming, that they wait for the winds to pick up and use the winds to gain altitude and fly over the storms. Eagles like and anticipate the storms because the storms give them more power in flight.[14] Similarly, there will be storms in your life. God will not prevent them, but His desire is that you hold onto Him. With God, you can fly higher than the storms, gaining power from their winds. Just imagine being safe in the Father's care and protection. Imagine being able to breathe deeply as He pushes you over the whirlwind of life. Not only are you covered by His wings, but you can fly on His wings, high above the trials.

Suggested Worship:

"Psalm 91 (On Eagles' Wings)" by Shane & Shane

Activation:

This activation may seem silly, but it is important. Grab a blanket and wrap it across your back and over your arms. The blanket is a symbol of God's wings. Sit down with your arms stretched wide and notice how your wings (blanket) form a perfect sanctuary for hiding. Notice that you could be on top of His wings when you fly high. Now close your eyes and imagine being safe under the Lord's wings.

Prayer: Lord, thank You for being my protector, my safe refuge. Thank You for taking me on Your wings and soaring above the stresses of this world. Lord, let's fly high today above my trials. Amen!

[14] "Flying Above the Storms." *Sermon Illustrator*, https://www.sermonillustrator.org/illustrator/sermon2/flying_above_the_storms.htm. Accessed 6 April 2022.

My Reflection:

3. The Lord Is Your Peace

Verses:

- *John 16:33 (NKJV):* "These things I have spoken to you, that in Me you may have peace. In the world you will have tribulation, but be of good cheer, I have overcome the world."
- *Philippians 4:7 (NIV):* "And the peace of God, which transcends all understanding, will guard your hearts and your minds in Christ Jesus."

God's Whisper:

Dear sweet child, I am flooding you with My peace today. I am here as a Rock for you, comforting you and loving you. I am here to wipe away your tears. I am here to bring you joy and laughter even in the midst of trials. Seek Me daily, and I will give you rest.

Personal:

I remember the first time I had peace that passes understanding, mentioned in Philippians 4:7. I heard the devastating news that my aunt had cancer while I was on vacation. I did the only thing I knew to do, which was to pray and read the Bible. Suddenly, after my quiet time, I had this wave of peace flood over me. God was saying He loved my aunt very much and He had her situation in His control. Sadly, my aunt passed away shortly thereafter even amid this amazing peace from God. It was a reassuring blessing to know she was home safe in Jesus' arms.

There are great struggles and devastating events we face here in this world. We don't always understand God's ways, yet we can stand firm and know God is in the midst of it all. He will give you peace and strategies to face each day. We need to remember that God's plans and ways are much greater than ours and remember He has overcome the world. Although it may not be easy some days, we need to call out to the Lord and give Him our burdens, and He will give us peace.

Suggested Worship:

"His Name Will Be" by River Valley Worship

Activation:

Grab a blanket, the heavier the better, and wrap it tight around your shoulders. Imagine the blanket is the Lord wrapping His arms around you. Pause and take a deep breath and rest in the Lord. He holds you in His arms.

Prayer: Lord, thank You for Your love for me and that You are the Prince of Peace. I call to You today and ask for Your peace, which passes all understanding. Help me to rely on Your perfect will today. Thank You, Jesus. Amen!

My Reflection:

4. The Promise Maker

Verses:

- *2 Corinthians 1:20 (NIV):* "For no matter how many promises God has made, they are 'Yes' in Christ. And so through him the 'Amen' is spoken by us to the glory of God."
- *Psalm 111:5 (TPT):* "He satisfies all who love and trust him, and he keeps every promise he makes."

God's Whisper:

I am the Way Maker, the Promise Keeper. Dear child, seek out My promises in My Word, the Bible. I list these promises for you to discover. Enjoy them and stand on these promises in both good and bad times. Boldly declare My promises when you feel defeated, for I am with you. My promises are true for you. I will raise you up and hold you firmly in My hand. Trust in Me and My promises.

Personal:

My husband and I have been part of a small group study at our church for years called The Promise Principle. The study starts with a prayer of surrender to the Lord and asks God to show us what He wants us to know. Next, we read a Bible chapter. It is suggested to focus on one chapter daily for the week to get a deeper meaning from the Lord. Next, we highlight a verse that has meaning from God for us, and then pray and meditate on the verse. We ask ourselves if the verse is a Promise, a Truth, or a Command; the verse can be one, two, or all three. We finish the study session by praying and thanking God for

His promises and truth for us. When in a small group setting, I have enjoyed hearing how God is speaking to others. I also have found when I incorporate these practices, the Lord opens my eyes to new promises.

Did you know the Bible has more than seven thousand promises from God to man? How amazing! All God's promises are yes and amen! Isaiah 55:11 says that God's word, or promises, will not return to Him void. God wants us to search out these promises that fill the Bible, for "it is the glory of God to conceal a matter; to search out a matter is the glory of kings (Proverbs 25:2, NIV). Pursue these promises with love, for God will show His love to those who passionately love Him (Proverbs 8:17a, TPT). Trust in the Lord, for He is faithful to fulfill His promises in His perfect timing.

Suggested Worship:

"Promises" by Micah and Jill Dillon

Activation:

Read Isaiah 45:3-7 aloud to the Lord and incorporate the Promise Principles outlined above.

Prayer: Lord, I am standing firm today in Your promises that are yes in Christ. I shout Amen to every promise. I am also standing on the promise of Your gift of perfect peace, and I won't let my heart will be troubled, nor will I be afraid (John 14:27, TPT). Thank You for all Your promises! I am asking You to help me discover Your promises for me each time I read the Bible. Amen!

My Reflection:

5. Your Resting Place

Verses:

- *Matthew 11:28-30 (NLT):* "Then Jesus said, 'Come to me, all of you who are weary and carry heavy burdens, and I will give you rest. Take my yoke upon you. Let me teach you, because I am humble and gentle at heart, and you will find rest for your souls. For my yoke is easy to bear, and the burden I give you is light.'"

God's Whisper:

Come here, My child. I know you are weary of the trials of this earth and heavy-laden from the earthly tasks before you. Come to Me, and I will give you rest. I will give you rest especially when your days are troubled and you don't know where to turn. Remember I am here for you. When your work is long and difficult and the burden of caring for your family lays heavy on your back, I am here for you. Come rest in Me, I will give you peace.

Personal:

I read a story by Joel S. Morton, a chaplain with the U.S. Navy,[15] where he talked about a carpenter who would touch a tree outside his home when he got home from work. When asked about it, he said, "Oh, that's my trouble tree. I know I can't stop having troubles out on the job, but one thing's for sure—my troubles don't belong in the house with my wife and children. So I just hang them up on the tree every night when I come

---

[15] Morton, Joel. "Hang Your Worries on a 'Trouble Tree.'" *Military News*, January 5, 2011, https://www.militarynews.com/norfolk-navy-flagship/news/chaplains_corner/hang-your-worries-on-a-trouble-tree/article_7c871ef9-646e-51d2-801d-81b95cec3056.html. Accessed 6 April 2022.

home. Then in the morning, I pick them up again. Funny thing is," he smiled, "when I come out in the morning to pick 'em up, they aren't nearly as many as I remember hanging up the night before."

I am reminded of great fears I had for my oldest son who was 19 at the time and lived over 1,000 miles away. His town was surrounded by great forest fires, and I feared for his life. Although I prayed for his safety, I didn't give all my worries to God and truly was nervous for days, unable to rest. Fast forward to this year when my son was in more tumultuous situations while away at sea with the Coast Guard. I was able to hand my worries more easily to the Lord, and I had great peace that God had my son in His protection. I had true peace and rest in the Lord.

Let Jesus be your "trouble tree." He can handle any burden and will make any troubles smaller and more manageable. Give all your burdens to Jesus today!

Suggested Worship:

"Rest with Me" by River Valley Worship

Activation:

I encourage you to go now and touch something outside your house that can represent your worry tree. It may be your front door, your mailbox, a fence, anything. Simply touch it and say, "God, I give You all my cares." He will take care of them and give you rest.

Prayer: Thank You, Lord for allowing me to rest in Your presence. I give You my thoughts of the craziness of my day. I give You the cares of my world and lay it at Your feet. I trust You will take care of every need. I trust You that I don't need to worry. Thank You for being my resting place. Amen!

My Reflection:

6. The Prince of Peace

AMY HIRSH

Verses:

- *Isaiah 9:6 (NIV):* "For to us a child is born, to us a son is given, and the government will be on his shoulders. And he will be called Wonderful Counselor, Mighty God, Everlasting Father, Prince of Peace."
- John 14:27 *(NLT):* "I am leaving you with a gift—peace of mind and heart. And the peace I give is a gift the world cannot give. So don't be troubled or afraid."

God's Whisper:

One of My most magnificent assignments as Messiah, is to bring wholeness and well-being to the world, including to YOU personally. As your Prince of Peace, I have the ability to replace your anxieties, doubts, fears, and burdens with My harmony, joy, a heart of gratitude, and true fulfillment. It's a gift you cannot receive anywhere in the world. Not from your job, not from a prestigious title, not from a better house, and certainly not from a bigger bank account. No, this peace is a supernatural gift that transcends all understanding. You only receive it when you choose to follow Me. Not only do you receive My peace when you follow Me, you now carry it onward! This means you are one of My peacemakers on earth! This is how My peace will continue to spread throughout the world until I return.

Personal:

I don't know about you, but a big weakness of mine is being prone to worry, especially about things out of my control, from bills and battles at work to struggles with relationships and issues with my kids. The list goes on, and if I'm not careful, my peace can evaporate before I finish my second cup of coffee. Thankfully, Jesus offers us a way out of the turmoil of troubling thoughts. If we cast our cares on Him, He promises to give us His peace. In Philippians 4:6-7 (NIV) Jesus says, "Do not be anxious about anything, but in every situation, by prayer and petition, with thanksgiving, present your requests to God. And the peace of God, which transcends understanding, will guard your hearts and minds in Christ Jesus." Now that's good news! So today, let the Prince of Peace transform you from worrier to warrior as you lay every care at His feet.

Suggested Worship:

"Peace" by We the Kingdom

Activation:

Today, surrender every burden in exchange for His peace. As soon as any anxious thought comes up, immediately tell Jesus, "I'm giving that to You, and in exchange, I receive Your peace." Thank Him for being your Prince of Peace. Ask Him to help you learn to guard your heart and mind against the troubles of this world and instead learn to abide in His harmony and wholeness.

Prayer: Jesus, I want to know You as my Prince of Peace. Help me to understand You can replace all my worries with peace of mind and harmony of heart. Thank You, Lord, for this gift that transcends understanding. Thank You, Lord, that I do not have to be troubled or afraid. Instead, I carry Your peace in Jesus' name. Amen!

My Reflection:

7. The Secret Place

Verse:

- *Psalm 25:14 (TPT):* "There's a private place reserved for the devoted lovers of Yahweh, where they sit near him and receive the revelation-secrets of his promises."

God's Whisper:

My child, war with Me in the secret place. Your secret place may be in your closet, your car, or in nature. Wherever you seek Me, you will find Me. My precious child, I long to have a special place where just you and I can meet, talk, and share. Be a prayer warrior for your family, friends, and neighbors. Call down victory from heaven. Call down love, call down peace from Me, and I will listen. I am eagerly waiting to hear from you today.

Personal:

Do you have a secret prayer room? A place you can go where no one disturbs you?

I have two favorite places, depending on the time of day, to escape and be with the Lord. My favorite morning place is in a small reading room. I love watching the sun rise while doing devotions, and then I pray. This time is special because it is before anyone else wakes up, and I hear the Lord more clearly. This is my secret place which is my most quiet place like found in Psalm 119:114 (TPT): "You're my place of quiet retreat, and your wraparound presence becomes my shield as I wrap myself in your Word!" At night, I relish the quiet of my closet. I feel I can war alongside God to take down strongholds in my family, city, or country. I feel it is my special place to be bold and "roar" against the enemy.

God is everywhere, but sometimes we can hear Him more clearly when we can retreat to a quiet, private place, perhaps one where we feel safe or can see something beautiful. If you don't have one yet, try to find one in your home, or even change some things around to create a new space.

Suggested Worship:

"The Door of Hope" by Kelly Outzen

Activation:

Look up the powerful 3-minute video on YouTube titled "War Room: Prayer Scene" by War Room Movie. After watching the video, find a quiet place to call out to the Lord and practice praying like the mighty warrior God created you to be.

Suggestions for a time in your secret place:

- Take a moment to focus your mind on God before you start and set the tone. I suggest you start by playing a worship song. God always loves praise and worship.
- Bring a pen and a copy of the Bible. Some people like to read Scripture on an electronic device, but I suggest your main source in your secret place be a hard copy so you can underline and highlight scriptures that have meaning for you, plus this will help you avoid distractions. I find it encouraging to review these notes when I read those scriptures at a later date and see how God spoke to me in the past.
- Be still and don't hurry in your quiet time, allowing God time to speak. Come to the feet of Jesus, put your burdens down, and ask Him to reveal secrets of His promises for you and your family today.

Prayer: Lord, I am calling out to You now. Raise me up to be a prayer warrior for You over my family. My heart's cry is for You, Lord. You can have my life, Lord—my will, my desires, I long to please only You. May I stand firm on Your precious word, today and forever. May I find and hear You today in my secret place with You, Lord. Amen!

My Reflection:

WEEK SEVEN

The God Who Whispers

What I tell you in the dark
speak in the daylight;
what is whispered in your ear,
proclaim from the roofs.

Matthew 10:27 (NIV)

1. The God Who Whispers

Verse:

- *Psalm 5:3 (NIV):* "In the morning, Lord, you hear my voice; in the morning I lay my requests before you and wait expectantly."

God's Whisper:

I am the Lord, Yahweh. I am the Great I Am. I love you, and I am here to be your Friend, your Confidant, your Father. Let Me whisper great and marvelous things to you today. I wish to bless you and give you peace and confidence in your life. Come closer to Me, dear child. Spend time with Me and worship Me. This glorifies Me and blesses you.

Personal:

God designed us to hear His still, small voice, His whisper. From Genesis, we know God talked and walked with Adam and Eve before the fall. Sadly, Satan came to destroy that unity. Jesus came that we may have unity and oneness with God once again. Trust you can and will hear from God. Know the enemy will bring doubt, but don't believe Satan's lies. God's words are never harsh, only loving, even if it is for correction. To grow your faith, when you hear God's whisper, write the words down so you will have a beautiful record to reflect on. You may hear a word, have a sense or impression of something, or even see an image. Some of the first words I heard from the Lord were so precious: "Smile, My child. Smile, for I am with you."

I was raised in a Christian home and have been a Christian since I was four. Yet I didn't understand until recently God could speak to me daily. Now I hear from God almost daily, and I long for you to hear as well! Psalm 62:5 (TPT) says, "I am standing in absolute stillness, silent before the one I love, waiting as long as it takes for him to rescue me. Only God is my Savior, and he will not fail me."

Suggested Worship:

"Whisper" by Jason Upton

Activation:

Proclaim Psalm 139:17 (NIV): "How precious to me are your thoughts, God! How vast is the sum of them!" Sit and listen to the Lord whisper to you. Have a pen and paper ready!

> **Prayer:** Dear Jesus, whisper to me today. My heart's cry is to give You glory, honor, and praise. I cannot fathom Your vastness. I am asking for You to whisper to me today. I love You, Lord. Amen!

My Reflection:

___

___

___

___

___

___

___

___

___

2. The Spirit of the Lord

Verses:

- *1 Samuel 10:6 (NIV):* "The Spirit of the Lord will come powerfully upon you, and you will prophesy with them, and you will be changed into a different person."
- *Isaiah 61:1 (NIV):* "The Spirit of the Sovereign Lord is on me, because the Lord has anointed me to proclaim good news to the poor. He has sent me to bind up the broken-hearted, to proclaim freedom for the captives and release from darkness for the prisoners."

God's Whisper:

As My spirit covers the earth, so shall you see My glory. My spirit rides the winds and waves. My spirit flies with butterflies and bees. I am everywhere. I am in every breath you take; I surround you. I am with you always. Come to Me and acknowledge Me today. I want to get to know you more. I want to share My heart with you. I want to share with you the great wonders of this world I created.

Personal:

On a chilly January morning, when few people dared to brave the beach, I walked there quietly and was in awe of God. All I could hear was the roar of the waves, and I could feel the wind on my face. The wind and the waves were all-encompassing. They were all I could focus on.

At high tide, watching wave after wave come ashore, I felt the Lord say, "I want to come closer to you, My friend." If we were to stand still and let His waves of love come, they would surround us and tenderly cover us. God's love is like that. All you have to do is stand still, not move at all; call to Him and be willing to get wet, and He will do the rest.

Cast your cares upon Him, my friend. He can handle them. His love for you is as vast as the ocean. He envelopes your cares and covers them in His love. When you walk away or get distracted from the source of love, which is God, you can't hear Him as well. But He is always near. Stay in His presence, always. Let Him draw you into His presence.

Suggested Worship:

"Hiraeth" by Clare Bell

Activation:

Set your timer for five minutes. Be still and rest, either lying down or seated. Close your eyes. Breathe deeply, and on your inhale say, "Holy Spirit;" on your exhale say "Breathe on me." Take notice and feel the Lord's presence. Breathe in His Spirit.

Prayer: Spirit of the one true God, fill me up with Your presence. Make me Your vessel to be used by You. Mend any brokenness in me so I can notice others who need Your love. Help me to love the brokenhearted. Thank You, Lord. I love You. Amen!

My Reflection:

3. God's Indescribable Beauty

Verses:

- *Revelation 4:3 (TPT):* "His appearance was *sparkling* like crystal and *glowing* like a carnelian gemstone. Surrounding the throne was a *circle of green light*, like an emerald rainbow."
- *Isaiah 6:3 (NIV):* "And they were calling to one another: 'Holy, holy, holy is the Lord Almighty; the whole earth is full of his glory.'"

God's Whisper:

My people don't confuse My sparkling glory for man's silly belief in gems. I created gems; I am more majestic than any gem on earth. Come and see My glory. I am above all creation. I am all colors, more than you have seen on earth. Close your eyes now and see My magnificence, My many colors of glory. Seek My face, and you will find My beauty.

Personal:

God created so much beauty all around us. We know from the book of Revelation that His appearance is spectacular and breathtaking. I can't wait to see how beautiful He and His magnificent throne room is. Sometimes I try to comprehend how amazing God and heaven will be like. I think of a crystal prism, rainbow lights brilliantly shining off it. I am mesmerized by the colors. So much color; so much brilliance! Most of the twenty-two chapters in Revelation refer to the throne of God, meaning the place God inhabits must be so incredible and more than we can comprehend. Imagine how amazing God's beauty is!

What joy we will have when we look at His face one day in heaven! We will erupt in praise. Equally exciting is the fact that we can seek His face here on earth and get a glimpse of His majesty! "When Handel [baroque composer] was asked how he had come to write Messiah, his answer was: 'I saw the heavens opened and God upon his great white throne.'"[16] Praising the Lord sets our hearts, minds, ears, and eyes on Him. Through praises, we can come up higher! Sing, praise, and shout for joy today, for the Lord is good and His glory fills the earth!

Suggested Worship:

"O Lord We Seek Your Face" by Worship Central NZ

Activation:

Locate or think of the most beautiful item around you, perhaps a painting, bouquet of flowers, or even a special piece of jewelry. Close your eyes and soak in the beauty of the item. Then imagine the Lord and how infinitely more beautiful He is! What a glorious sight!

Prayer: Oh, the beauty of Your face, Lord, is all I seek. May You reveal Yourself to me so I can gaze at Your sparkling beauty today. May I rest in Your glorious presence today. Amen!

---

[16] Barclay, William. "The Opening Heavens And The Opening Door – Revelation 4:1." *Bible Portal*, https://bibleportal.com/commentary/section/william-barclay/the-opening-heavens-and-the-opening-door-revelation-41-8900. Accessed 10 November 2022.

My Reflection:

4. Jesus Is the Light in the Darkness

Verses:

- *John 8:12 (NIV):* "When Jesus spoke again to the people, he said, 'I am the light of the world. Whoever follows me will never walk in darkness, but will have the light of life.'"
- *John 1:5 (TPT):* "And this Light never fails to shine through the darkness—Light that darkness could not overcome!"

God's Whisper:

I am here shining brightly for all to see, My child. Lift up your head and look for Me today. I am bursting through the darkness of your world. My light unearths all darkness, and with My light comes healing. Come to Me, dear sweet child, and know that revealing the darkness within you is good, and I will be there to comfort you. For in the light, goodness grows, gardens grow, and kindness grows.

Personal:

In the past when I've pictured Jesus as a light of the world, candlelight would come to mind. But He is not a small candlelight. Jesus is brighter than the sun! Jesus is a Bursting Force of Light in the darkness! Jesus is breaking every chain and lifting every weight holding you down. He is here to shine brightly for all to see. He came down into darkness on earth because He loves you—He loves YOU! Have faith, dear friend. Jesus is the light shining for you even if it feels like you are in a dark tunnel now.

Breathe deep, reach out, and rest in Jesus today.

When my boys started school, my nightly prayer would be that they would be a light shining for Jesus wherever they went. I would tell them specifics of keeping their chins up as they walked the halls at school and smiling at people they walked past. I would remind them to invite people to their table at lunch who didn't have a place to sit and looked lonely. I found out that in high school my oldest son befriended someone. A simple act of saying hi during class led this person to quickly become part of a small friend group. This act changed the trajectory of this person's life, who felt accepted. When you make even a small effort to let Jesus's light shine through you, you will be amazed at what will happen.

Suggested Worship:

"Let There Be Light" by Bryan and Katie Torwalt

Activation:

Be the light for Jesus today and spread kindness to those around you. Ask Jesus who needs a special word of encouragement. Send the person a short note or text right now saying you are thinking of them and that Jesus loves them.

Prayer: Lord, help me to be a light shining for You in this dark world. I choose to follow You today. As Your word says, I will never walk in darkness again. Thank You! Lord, please open my eyes to those hurting around me today and let me be a light for You. Amen!

My Reflection:

5. You Are God's Heir

Verses:

- *Galatians 3:29 (NIV):* "If you belong to Christ, then you are Abraham's seed, and heirs according to the promise."
- *Colossians 1:12 (NIV):* "Giving joyful thanks to the Father, who has qualified you to share in the inheritance of his holy people in the kingdom of light."

God's Whisper:

I sent My Son to save you, My child. If you were the only person to reach out and believe in Me, I still would have sent My Son to die for you so you could be with Me in heaven. I love you so much. Peace I give you. Love I send you today. My child, do not wait to come to Me, come to Me now. You are My heir, dear child, a child of mine with inexorable riches. Come discover with Me all I have waiting for you: freedom, peace, love, and joy! I am always here waiting to meet with you; spend time with Me daily.

Personal:

Jesus died and gave His life for you and me on the cross; just before Jesus died, He said "It is finished!" (John 19:30, NKJV). This means the debt is paid in full. Our debt, being our sins, no longer needs an animal sacrifice to cleanse us so that we can be in God's presence. His death freed us from this debt. Jesus' work on earth was completed that day to save people from their sins. His blood protects us, provides for us, and gives us eternal life with Him in heaven. His death provided everything we need. We need to speak this truth—it is powerful to speak out loud.

Jesus' blood is the bridge that crossed a great divide. Jesus made a way where there was no way. We don't have to go through anyone else to talk to God as people did in the Old Testament; we all have the opportunity to directly come to God. Always remember you are a child of the King, the Most-High God. You are valued as an heir *now*, my friend, not in the future. In Romans 8:17 we learn we are heirs of God and co-heirs with Christ, that we have been given authority and the true birth-right "if indeed we share in his sufferings in order that we may also share in his glory" (NIV). Grab hold of your inheritance today.

Suggested Worship:

"How He Loves" by David Crowder Band

Activation:

Read John 3:16-17. Replace the word "world" with your name. Now read the passage again and let the significance of the Lord's love for you sink in.

Prayer: Father God, thank You for sending Your precious Son Jesus to die for me. I am so humbled and in awe of the sacrifice of Your Son. Today I acknowledge and claim my birthright as Your heir and command victory over the evil around me. May I remember Your great love for me, and may I be a light shining for You in this world today. Amen!

My Reflection:

6. *Abba Father*

with TERESA DAVIS

Verses:

- *Galatians 4:6 (NIV):* "Because you are his sons, God sent the Spirit of his Son into our hearts, the Spirit who calls out, '*Abba*, Father.'"
- *Mark 11:24 (NKJV):* "Therefore I say to you, whatever things you ask when you pray, believe that you receive *them*, and you will have *them*."

God's Whisper:

I am here, My child, cry out to Me now. I want to welcome you into My presence. Sit with Me and hear Me. Hear My whisper. I am calling you. My heart's cry is for you to know Me and know I am a good, good Father. I want you to see, hear, and feel My presence. Come running to Me. I will catch you as you fall into My arms. I will carry you today. I am waiting for you now. Reach out to Me.

Personal:

One winter day when I was going to feed the birds in my backyard, I was overwhelmed, realizing that no matter what, the birds would show up to eat. They don't wonder whether I am going to put out food; they just come! They don't worry if there will be enough; they just come! This is how we are to be as believers. We are to be expectant. Be expectant for what the Lord Abba Father has for you. He is a good, good Father and longs to feed your body, mind, and soul with goodness. His mercies are rich and abundant. As Matthew 6:26 says, "Look at the birds of the air; they do not sow or reap or store away in barns, and yet your heavenly Father feeds them. Are you not much more valuable than they?" (NIV).

Suggested Worship:

"Abba" by Jonathan Helser

Activation:

Write a letter to your Abba Father. Tell Him your heart, your hurts, sorrows, and joys. Tell Him how much you love Him.

Prayer: Spirit of the one true God, I call to You now. Thank You for being here with me today. Thank You for loving me and caring for me so deeply. I am thankful You care for my every need even if I don't ask for it. You always know what I need. Thank You for completely knowing me and loving me even in my weakness. I open my arms and welcome You today. I am running to You now, Father. I love You, Lord. Amen!

My Reflection:

7. Holy Fire

Verse:

- *Matthew 3:11 (TPT):* "Those who repent I baptize with water, but there is coming a man after me who is more powerful than I. In fact, I'm not even worthy enough to pick up his sandals. He will submerge you into union with the Spirit of Holiness and with a raging fire!"

God's Whisper:

My Holy Fire will fall on you, My child, if you ask for it. The blazing hot fire of My Holy Spirit purifies and ignites My people to flourish for My kingdom. I desire to give you this perfect fire from Me. Call on Me now. I long to fill you, cleanse you, and refine you with My Fire.

Personal:

Have you ever been filled with God's Holy Fire? It is amazing! I love The Passion Translation version of Matthew 3:11, which speaks of submerging you in His raging fire. What a vision! Once you have been hit with the fire of God, nothing else matters, only Jesus.

I longed to be filled with Holy Fire for years. I would eagerly seek the Lord, asking for fresh fire, but still not experiencing the infilling of the Holy Ghost that I saw others experience. I am not sure why the Lord waited to flow His fire over me; probably because He wanted me to stop trying to control His will while growing me in the waiting period and learning to seek Him first. It was a four-year journey of healing and learning, one I am grateful for now. I believe my journey is a big reason why I wrote this book.

I have a sense from the Lord that we are entering a season where God's Holy Fire is falling easier on those who humbly ask. I see the body of Christ running after God's will; they are going deeper now than I have seen before, and faith in Christ is rising. I believe God desires our hunger for Him and that when we ask God for Holy Fire, He will deliver it.

I know you, dear friend, are hungry for God. After all, you have been here with me for seven weeks learning more of God's heart for you along the way! My heart's desire is for you to experience His Holy Fire today! May His raging fire purify and burn brightly in you today.

Suggested Worship:

"Fresh Fire" featuring Brandon Lake & Naomi Raine and Maverick City Music by TRIBL records

Activation:

Find a quiet space, settle your heart, and worship the Lord. Ask for God's Holy Fire to fall on you. Jesus said in Matthew 7:8 (NIV), "For everyone who asks receives; the one who seeks finds; and to the one who knocks, the door will be opened." Be bold and declare you want God's glory and fire to fall on you. He will send it. His fire will cleanse you, heal your heart, and bring you closer to Him. Find like-minded people who long for God's fire and pray together. Follow strong believers who have God's incredible anointing and who can guide you in new ways to grow closer with Him.

Prayer: Oh Lord, I desire Your Holy Fire to fall on me now. I desire Your fire deeply burning in my soul. Come purify me, Father, and fill me with Your fire so all can see You burning brightly through me. I am asking for more of You today! Thank You for Your pure love for me. Amen!

My Reflection:

Final Thoughts and Prayer

Final Thoughts:

Dear friend, I pray you encountered the heart of God and heard His whisper to you on this seven-week journey. May this journey catapult you into a new wonder of the Lord and a deeper desire to know Him in a more personal way. I pray the following scripture over you found in Colossians 2:2-3 (TPT): "I am contending for you that your hearts will be wrapped in the comfort of heaven and woven together into love's fabric. This will give you access to all the riches of God as you experience the revelation of God's great mystery—Christ. For our spiritual wealth is in him, like hidden treasure waiting to be discovered—heaven's wisdom and endless riches of revelation knowledge." Go boldly into your day, dear friend, boldly knowing the Lord loves you. Be confident you are hearing His whisper for you.

Activation:

Take some time to write a personal letter to God, thanking Him for what He has shown you over the past seven weeks.

Prayer: Lord, thank You for Your love for me and for Your whispers over me. May I be reminded today to look for You in the details around me. Let Your spirit flow fresh on me today and embolden me to share Your love with others. Amen!

Dear Lord:

Prayer Requests

Date	REQUEST	Date Answered

"One day Jesus taught the apostles to keep praying and never stop or lose hope."

Luke 18:1 (TPT)

Prayer Requests

Date	REQUESTS	Date Answered

"Answer me when I call, O God of my righteousness! You have given me relief when I was in distress. Be gracious to me and hear my prayer!"

Psalm 4:1 (ESV)

Prayer Requests

Date	REQUESTS	Date Answered

"Therefore I tell you, whatever you ask for in prayer, believe that you have received it, and it will be yours."

Mark 11:24 (NIV)

ABOUT THE AUTHOR:

Christa Joy Spaeth: Christa is a Minnesota-based author who is passionate about fulfilling her purpose to help the hurting and share the love of Christ. She longs for everyone to have "God encounters" and to hear His whisper. Christa is a wife to an incredible man of God, mom to two young men who love the Lord, and an entrepreneur. She knows God called her to ministry and His promises are being fulfilled!

You can connect with Christa at christajoyministries@gmail.com or www.christajoyministries.com.

ABOUT THE CONTRIBUTORS:

Teresa Davis: Teresa loves people and is an immediate friend to anyone she meets. Her passion is to share the awe and wonder of God's heart with everyone.

Amy Hirsh: Amy has a deep passion for family and considers her role as a wife and mother to her three children to be her primary ministry. In addition to serving her tribe, Amy has a heart for storytelling and encouraging women through media. She has held many media roles including news anchor, home shopping host, and brand ambassador.

Teresa Krafft: The Lord has given Teresa and her husband, Tom, a passion to equip leaders for Kingdom work. To learn more and sign up for a free account, visit www.reliht.com.

Kristin Kurtz: Kristin is a life and holistic health coach. Kristin carries keys of revelation to unlock breakthrough in the body. You can email her at kristinkurtz@newwingscoaching.net or visit her website at www.newwingscoaching.net.

Krystal Rasmussen: Krystal and her husband, Jeff, have three children and reside in Nebraska. She is a seer prophet with a heart to raise up prophetic voices that carry the heart of the Father.

Leslie Schewe: Leslie is a homeschooling mom of three. She is a worshiper. She has a godly marriage and is a parenting advocate.

WORSHIP MUSIC REFERENCES:

Ark Creative. "Life Giver." YouTube. https://www.youtube.com/watch?v=bPnTlh9SHQg.

Awakening Music. "Jesus Lover of My Soul." YouTube. https://www.youtube.com/watch?v=jDZcBJlH0vM.

Bell, Clare. "Hiraeth." YouTube. https://www.youtube.com/watch?v=4gE3iQev_kQ.

Bell, Clare. "Lord you have my heart (& Spontaneous Worship)." YouTube. https://www.youtube.com/watch?v=T9m57m3D_ho.

Bell, Clare. "Spacious Place." YouTube. https://www.youtube.com/watch?v=zqAaEnFF-SQ.

Campbell, Jervis. "Glory." YouTube. https://www.youtube.com/watch?v=x59Si20PqPE.

Carnes, Cody. Jobe, Kari. "The Blessing." YouTube. https://www.youtube.com/watch?v=Zp6aygmvzM4.

Cook, Amanda. "Shepherd." YouTube. https://www.youtube.com/watch?v=bVjedGudN8w.

David Crowder Band. "How He Loves." YouTube. https://www.youtube.com/watch?v=SUKJEhkk2G8. "How He Loves" written by John Mark McMillan. © 2005 Integrity's Hosanna! Music (ASCAP) (adm at IntegratedRights.com). All rights reserved. Used by permission.

Dillon, Micah. "Joy of the Lord." YouTube. https://www.youtube.com/watch?v=hkcdwXh8K38.

Dillon, Micah. "More than Enough." YouTube. https://www.youtube.com/watch?v=HYSnP4PZbJ0.

Dillon, Jill. Dillon, Micah. "Promises." YouTube. https://www.youtube.com/watch?v=f2u9B5qlduU.

Gayle, Charity. "I Speak Jesus." YouTube. https://www.youtube.com/watch?v=PcmqSfr1ENY.

Gretzinger, Steffany. "You Know Me." YouTube. https://www.youtube.com/watch?v=-h9wpvwAF-M.

Hart Pearsons, Sarah. "Nothing but the Blood, O the Blood of Jesus." YouTube. https://www.youtube.com/watch?v=3V1OJ0daJWQ&t=181s.

Harvester Worship. "Set Apart." YouTube. https://www.youtube.com/watch?v=UkUaMGeQ0B0.

Helser, Jonathan. "Abba" YouTube. https://www.youtube.com/watch?v=ehz9a1BqnCA.

I AM THEY. "Crown Him." YouTube. https://www.youtube.com/watch?v=HFq96fWBnrs.

Jesus Culture. "Defender." YouTube. https://www.youtube.com/watch?v=DtPgAFpkJLE.

Jesus Culture. "More than Enough." YouTube. https://www.youtube.com/watch?v=In57dBbbonk.

Jobe, Kari. "The Garden." YouTube. https://www.youtube.com/watch?v=Y43Z0WJLDS4.

Lake, Brandon. Raine, Naomi. "Fresh Fire." YouTube. https://www.youtube.com/watch?v=9jDLBpvcjg0.

McDowell, William. Zschech, Darlene. "Way Maker." YouTube. https://www.youtube.com/watch?v=ulFK2tv4GWQ.

Orenze, Victoria. "You are my Hiding Place." YouTube. https://www.youtube.com/watch?v=G-iRbce8bto.

Outzen, Kelly. "The Door of Hope." YouTube. https://www.youtube.com/watch?v=GzGfuYMk_-Q.

Outzen, Kelly. "The God of Angel Armies." YouTube. https://www.youtube.com/watch?v=i0LGzUG3Ke4.

Papa, Matt. "The Lord is a Warrior." YouTube. https://www.youtube.com/watch?v=_D9MmqnQs8w.

River Valley Worship. "East to West." YouTube. https://www.youtube.com/watch?v=cUf4Jr8MBuU.

River Valley Worship. "His Name will Be." YouTube. https://www.youtube.com/watch?v=zLc85emkm-Q.

River Valley Worship. "Rest with Me." YouTube. https://www.youtube.com/watch?v=D9x9et3hVWU.

River Valley Worship. "Sanctuary." YouTube. https://www.youtube.com/watch?v=DoAn8fzCNuU.

Scrimale, Amanda. "Healing is Coming (Habakkuk's Prayer)." YouTube. https://www.youtube.com/watch?v=i2gv_dF3Yus.

Shane & Shane. "Holy, Holy, Holy (We Bow Before Thee)." YouTube. https://www.youtube.com/watch?v=sl6ZkTbUgW4.

Shane & Shane. "Psalm 139 (Far too Wonderful)." YouTube. https://www.youtube.com/watch?v=dIWMXiT8yrs.

Shane & Shane. "Psalm 8 (How Majestic Is Your Name)." YouTube. https://www.youtube.com/watch?v=bPSv8vredVs.

Shane & Shane. "Psalm 91 (On Eagles' Wings)." YouTube. https://www.youtube.com/watch?v=c0t3w9ZYsTo.

The Rock, The Road, and The Rabbi Foundation. "The God Who Sees." YouTube. https://www.youtube.com/watch?v=sz81dlfwf4Y.

Torwalt, Bryan. Torwalt Katie. "Canvas and Clay." YouTube. https://www.youtube.com/watch?v=fcdGL4pzmsE.

Torwalt, Bryan. Torwalt, Katie. "Flame of Fire, Rushing Wind." YouTube. https://www.youtube.com/watch?v=BKfSMX-LdWg.

Torwalt, Bryan. Torwalt, Katie. "Let There Be Light." YouTube. https://www.youtube.com/watch?v=EyMAACDZuoU.

Upton, Jason. "Whisper." YouTube. https://www.youtube.com/watch?v=eD_xQNhBlfM. "Whisper" written by Ben Smith & Jason Upton, © 2014 Key Of David Music (adm at IntegratedRights.com). All rights reserved. Used by permission.

Walker-Smith, Kim. "Protector." YouTube. https://www.youtube.com/watch?v=laZvXrnpSEc.

Waterman, Roma. "20 minute deep prayer music l Prophetic Worship l Spontaneous Song l 'Rivers of Healing.'" YouTube. https://www.youtube.com/watch?v=-CKwAMEyPIQ.

Waterman, Roma. "Not My Battle." YouTube. https://www.youtube.com/watch?v=OgSvXBTzMPM.

War Room Movie. "War Room: Prayer Scene." YouTube. https://www.youtube.com/watch?v=_WpfkFyG5qQ&list=PLbNDs4Vt_NCzRqvpMFe0By2uqXDTCXMv0.

We the Kingdom. "Peace." YouTube. https://www.youtube.com/watch?v=dMzavY9lgLM.

Wells, Tauren. "God's Not Done with You." YouTube. https://www.youtube.com/watch?v=cVHrkYBEgFM.

Wickham, Phil. "Battle Belongs." YouTube. https://www.youtube.com/watch?v=johgSkNj3-A.

Williams, Zach. "Rescue Story." YouTube. https://www.youtube.com/watch?v=9Yr48Berkqc.

Worship Central NZ. "O Lord We Seek Your Face." YouTube. https://www.youtube.com/watch?v=i-4Q4kXfv84.

You, YoungMin. "If Jireh by Elevation Worship was a Piano Solo." YouTube. https://www.youtube.com/watch?v=FOas-EbWD2I.